Through Grown-up Eyes

Living With Childhood Fame

Robert Henrey

ISBN HB 978-0-9570481-7-1
ISBN 978-0-9570481-8-8

A catalogue record for this book is available from the British Library

Published in Great Britain
in 2013 by
Polperro Heritage Press
Clifton-upon-Teme, Worcestershire WR6 6EN UK
www.polperro.press.co.uk

Cover design: Steve Bowgen

Printed by
Orphans Press
Leominster, Herefordshire
United Kingdom

Can you keep a secret?

I can't...
and there's
trouble,
maybe
murder,
whatever
that is...

BOBBY HENREY
who gives
what LIFE,
quoting critics,
calls "an absolutely
staggering perform-
ance by an 8-year-old"
in **CAROL REED'S**
four-award thriller
THE FALLEN IDOL

presented by **DAVID O. SELZNICK**
produced and directed by
CAROL REED
written by **GRAHAM GREENE**
starring **RALPH RICHARDSON**
MICHELE MORGAN
with
SONIA DRESDEL
DENIS O'DEA
JACK HAWKINS
and introducing
BOBBY HENREY
an SRO release

1948 publicity poster

Contents

Introduction

At the age of eight, something curious happened to me. It was so curious and so out-of-the-ordinary that I did not even find surprising the unusual sequence of events which led to it coming about. I just accepted it for what it was – something that came out of the blue, belonging to a world so wholly outside my experience that I simply could not have conceived of any of this happening before it actually happened.

In the many years that have since gone by, I have often been asked whether I now wish this quite extraordinary passage of events had never taken place. That, to me at least, is not a meaningful question. It was something over which I had absolutely no say. It just happened. It did, of course, fall to me to deal with the complexity of its unintended consequences. Is that not, however, the way things are with so many of life's great surprises? We are simply left to cope with the great tumble of confusion that is of their making.

What I do remember, though, is that everything happened very quickly. It was June 1947 and, it being my eighth birthday, my grandmother had just made more of a fuss of me than usual. I loved my grandmother with an intensity that had perhaps much to do with the fact that I was an only child. She had become my great protector against the injustices of the world.

So there I was, messing around with the chickens, ducks and rabbits she kept and lovingly nurtured in the grassy courtyard behind the ancient Normandy farmhouse which was our home. I think I already suspected a truth that I would later come to know with blinding certainty: this place, seen through my child-like eyes, was magic indeed. There would be other glimpses of paradise but this would prove to be the first of them all and, brief as it would inevitably turn out to be, the longest lasting and closest to perfection.

The next day my mother arrived – quite unexpectedly – from England and announced that she and I would be flying from nearby Deauville in a special plane to London so I could meet some people who wanted to make a film. I remember much more about the flight than about anything else. This was the first time I had stepped into an aeroplane. I can still hear and feel the droning of the engines, smell the slight whiff of aviation fuel, and feel the rush of cool air, as the small prop made its ascent over the fields and woods of France. Everything looked quite different to me: the brown spotted cows were mere specks. The plane banked heading up north, away from the Norman coast, and into the dark blue beyond that was the English Channel. I remember feeling not just excited but also extraordinarily lucky. That feeling has remained with me. I am an inveterate traveller and I still relish the idea of peering from the outside into worlds that my senses would otherwise never have experienced. I was much more interested in the flight than in the audition that followed it.

Actually I do not think it was much of an audition.

My father had always worked in London so there he was waiting for us when the little plane landed on the other side of the Channel. The three of us were ushered into a solemn looking black chauffeur-driven car, something else that struck me as extraordinarily unusual. My parents had never owned a car and we were not used to being driven around – other than very occasionally in one of those big lumbering taxis that, the war now over, were to be seen all over London.

We were driven to an office in Hyde Park Corner that was within walking distance of our London flat. There were several men in suits who smiled a lot – at least when they talked to me – and asked questions. As far as I was concerned there was nothing to it. I was, however, impressed by the size of this office. Unlike our Mayfair flat it was huge beyond belief and instead of overlooking a dingy courtyard, it faced the park. Much later I learned that within this great mansion of an office we had been treated to lunch and that among those at that lunch was Carol Reed, who had already made an enviable reputation for himself as a film director. This same Carol Reed was the one who had apparently asked the most questions, and then still more strangers had appeared and taken photographs – of me, I suppose, but I remember nothing about what I was asked. The flash of the cameras made more of an impression.

My parents, who by now had taken up the habit of writing about pretty much anything and everything that happened to them, were, so they wrote later, quite awed by the spectacle of all this extravagant luxury. Britain was, after all, still recovering slowly and painfully from the war years so that the good things of life – including the ingredients that went into a decent meal – were still measured out by way of colour-coded coupons issued in ration books bearing the royal coat of arms. These kind of restrictions apparently did not apply to film impresarios – or so it seemed. The world, though, as I would learn much later, was indeed changing. His Majesty King George VI would, within a matter of weeks, cease to reign as Emperor of India.

When the time for questions and for picture taking was over my mother took me back to Normandy – in the same little plane the film impresarios had so extravagantly sent to fetch me. My father stayed behind in London so he could go to his own office somewhere in Fleet Street; one that was assuredly not wood panelled and certainly not the kind where lunch was served from silver trays.

As for me, I remember the delight of being back with my grandmother. The chickens were, as always, busy digging up worms in the garden. The luxury of being unconcerned with anything other than the present is a joy beyond compare.

When, in time, my mother told me I would be acting in a film and that this would take up the best part of several months, I assumed that unexpected things like this simply happened and that there was nothing very much I or anyone else could do about it. I had little awareness of how other children actually lived.

1

The Ancient House Of My Birth

The ancient Norman house of my birth, set on a hill overlooking Villers-sur-Mer just west of Deauville, has always been part of my consciousness. I have, since earliest childhood, been aware of its antiquity. Downstairs, set within the stonework of one of the fireplaces, is a small marble tile into which the year 1555 has been engraved. That is it; no inscription; no clue as to who inserted it into the headstone to the left of the fireplace and not the slightest hint as to whether the date refers to the construction of the fireplace itself, or to the two-storied half timbered frame that was erected around it, or even to the thick stone walls at the other end of the house that might conceivably be older than anything else still standing. There are no ancestral archives to which I might refer and for good reason, since my father acquired the house in 1937, 'on a whim', as my mother was in the habit of saying with a hint of sarcasm.

The seller was a flamboyant local businessman who dabbled in real estate. I remember him because, much later, after the war, he and my father had taken a liking to each other and he would invite us to lunch. He was still wheeling and dealing and I thought of him as immensely rich – understandably since, seen through my childish eyes, those lunches were magnificent affairs attended by a cook and a servant girl in a bonnet. What he had sold to my father – a charming but inexperienced city dweller – was just a very old house standing in the middle of a soggy field in Normandy. A tenant farmer, his wife and their children lived it in. It had no electricity, no telephone and no plumbing of any sort. There was, however, a stream at the bottom of the field. Someone had erected a lean-to barn against the house's northern wall – a space to store hay and to milk cows during the winter months. Brown and white Norman cows, pigs and chickens coexisted with the farmer and his family.

My father, Robert Henrey, a journalist living in London with my mother, Madeleine, was charmed. They had little money to spare but apparently just enough to buy the house, the 30 or so acres on which the farmer grazed his cows and then fix it up.

My father was English by birth. His own father, Selby Henrey, was a highly dignified but impoverished clergyman who had married a wealthy and aristocratic wife, Euphemia. She, notwithstanding her strict adherence to the ascetic principles befitting life in a vicarage in suburban London, had arranged for her children to be tutored by a French governess. This turned out to have had a profound influence on my father's life. The governess was from Falaise, a Norman town destined to play one of the star roles in the history of the English speaking peoples, for it was there that William the Conqueror's father took a fancy to a winsome local lass and sired a bastard son who would grow up to have immense charm, physical resilience, and huge territorial ambitions.

The governess must have been a powerful storyteller for she not only taught my father to speak near-flawless French but also imbued him with a fascination for this lush province known for its cider apples and brown spotted cows. It must also have been largely thanks to her influence that my father, as a young journalist practising his trade in London, met and fell in love with my mother. She was born in Paris, spoke English haltingly and worked as a manicurist in a fashionable London hotel. In Paris my mother had known grinding poverty: her father Émile was a bricklayer and her mother, Matilda, a seamstress. After her father's premature death – he caught pneumonia and died a few days thereafter – she and her mother came to London in hope of a better life. My mother had no formal education beyond middle school but by all accounts was stunningly attractive. By marrying her, my father had opened up to her a world that would have otherwise been totally beyond her reach. It also became abundantly clear that she was highly intelligent and a gifted storyteller.

My parents spent their early-married life in London. As far as my father was concerned, London was the best place on earth to be a journalist. So why did he embark on this Norman adventure? This was certainly not something my mother had dreamt up. She had grown to love London and had no ties to Normandy. Her mother Matilda – my beloved French grandmother – was from the Loire Valley and my grandfather from Provence where his humble ancestors had mined the coal seams near the Roman town of Nîmes.

The dream was clearly my father's: a Norman farm not too far from

London and, I think most importantly, a place to raise a child. I suspect that it was the anticipation of my conception that drove my father to indulge a dream that was very much his. My mother, as I came to know her, was a strong willed, independently minded woman who never hesitated to speak her mind – often with barbed precision. I have every reason to believe that she and my father did not see eye-to-eye on the matter of the Normandy idyll. I am not sure why she gave in but she did so perhaps because she sensed that this was indeed an adventure and that she and my father could not go on living in a cramped London flat for the rest of their lives. She was 31 at the time and could not have known that the decision would have a profound effect on her mother's life and that she herself would in time become fiercely attached to the place my father had fallen in love with.

In that summer of 1937, the place did indeed need fixing up. Besides the tenant farmer, his wife, and three children, it sheltered cows, chickens and pigs. There were a few goats, a horse, maybe even two horses, and a donkey. There were no tractors or automobiles in those days – certainly not on a Norman farm as small as this one – so stocky carthorses were essential to haymaking and to all kinds of carting. The donkey came in handy for milking. The cows had to be milked mornings and evenings. The farmer and his wife, and those of their children old enough to help out, trudged out to whichever of the fields the cows happened to be grazing, taking with them buckets and three-legged stools. No one in their wildest dreams could have foreseen the advent of milking machines and milking parlours. There were no electric power lines reaching up to the little farm and the thought of an independent generator just had not made its way to this part of the world. The donkey carried the churns – two on each side of its saddle. The return trip was rough on the donkey. It rains a lot in Normandy and even the best fields muddy up to the point where the hooves make a swishing, sucking sound. I was to become quite familiar with the bray of a donkey – an extraordinarily loud protest out of all proportion to the actual size of the animal.

So the suave and charming real estate broker – Victor was his name – had warned my father about the need to fix things up before moving in. It was excellent advice, but it turned out to be unexpectedly challenging.

Victor, or Toto for short, had also made a deal with the tenants. They would move themselves, plus cows, pigs, chickens, goats, horses and ass out of the way, but only on condition that the new owner provide them with a newly-built house and stables. The deal was sensible enough but my father, unwittingly, made what turned out to be a mistake: not one with long-lasting consequences but a serious mistake nonetheless. He thought it would be a fine idea to erect the new buildings close to the existing house: close enough to form a picturesque three-sided barnyard. That was the way Norman farmsteads had been built over the centuries: the haylofts and cowsheds adjacent to where the people lived. There were charmingly illustrated 19th century engravings of Norman farmsteads to prove it.

It was the proximity of the farmer and his querulous family, not so much that of his smelly pigs, chickens, ducks, horses, donkey and lowing cows that turned out to be the undoing of the arrangement. My father, accustomed to the relative gentility of living in a flat on the Brompton Road, within walking distance of Harrods, had neglected to take into account the human element.

Be that as it may, my father – under Toto's tutelage – went to work hiring a local contractor so the new house and adjacent stables could be built as quickly as possible. It turned out to be a sturdy, rather boxy design which included an open fireplace but otherwise had no frills. No frills except that my father opted for a thatched roof: incongruously, given the modernity of the new structure's stucco-covered concrete walls. The farmer and his family were expected to make do with three rooms – plus a narrow kitchen, a privy with indoor plumbing and a dairy with running water. Farmhouses always included a dairy: a room for skimming cream off fresh milk and then turning the cream into butter with a hand operated churn – a job invariably given to children. Whenever I smell curdled milk, I experience a Proustian recollection of things past: the rancid odours that wafted from the dairies of the farmhouses of my Norman childhood: odours mixed with the acrid smell of soot-laden smoke escaping from open fireplaces and kitchen stoves.

The destiny of the new house was that it would be referred to as the cottage, in French as well as in English. In French the word has a decidedly English ring to it. I think of a cottage as being old and quaint. It was neither, notwithstanding its thatched roof, but the name has withstood the test of time. The fact is that over the years, well after the farmers for whom it had been built disappeared, we grew increasingly fond of it. To me, to my wife and then to our children, it served during our vacations as a place we could call our own. It was also a welcome refuge from whatever might be happening in the ancient farmhouse. With time, the new has blended gracefully with its surroundings as if the ancient farmhouse had graciously made room for it.

The farmers displaced from the ancient farmhouse were supposed to be better off in the cottage, particularly since they now had running water. My father had commissioned the digging of a well – this was considered to be quite a feat since it was a good 60 feet deep – and installed a petrol pump with enough power to fill storage tanks inside the attics of both houses, the ancient and the modern. It is not clear that the farmer shared my father's enthusiasm for this innovation. I also suspect that the cottage with its concrete walls felt a lot colder in winter than did the half-timbering of the ancient farmhouse and that he felt short-changed by the move. He certainly made much of the fact that the new fireplace smoked and contributed to the draughtiness of his family's living quarters. Normans are notoriously hard to please; or so thought my parents, echoing a widely held belief.

My father asked the builders to incorporate into the cottage's chimneystack a large plaque with a date: August 13th 1938. This was in fact my mother's 32nd birthday and I suspect that the date bears only a vague relationship to when the construction work was actually completed. As I grew up, I became aware of the fact that my father did such things. He liked placing my mother on a pedestal and did so frequently. It was a habit I found puzzling and somewhat irksome. After a very long while, I came up with an explanation that served to remind me of the complexity of my parents' relationship. My explanation rested on an interpretation of the myth of Pygmalion that had so famously inspired George Bernard Shaw to conceive of the story which became the film *My Fair Lady*. It was the myth of the sculptor who fell in love with his own creation, but then had to deal with the reality that she had a mind of her own.

With the farmers out of the ancient farmhouse, my father now set about the serious business of making it suitable to be lived in. It was an awesome task. In common with many traditional Norman houses it had a mud floor or, to be more precise, a clay floor. This is a part of Normandy where good quality clay is readily available and, so long as it is kept dry, it does a fine job providing insulation and durability. When a clay floor wears down, it can be repaired expeditiously. Be that as it may, my parents were not about to continue this particular tradition and the builders laid a proper tile floor – a black and white checker board. Clay had other uses having, since time immemorial, been mixed with chopped up straw and plastered in between the timbers holding up the walls. That was something else my parents would change. The builders replaced the wattle and daub between the timbers with plaster. They actually covered most of the interior walls with liberally applied layers of plaster, hiding the ancient timbers and stonework but providing insulation against Normandy's notoriously rainy and windy weather. The roof was also in need of serious repair. Traditional Norman roofs were thatched. Thatchers were skilled craftsmen adept at energetically packing down straw and securing it to wooden laths with the help of heavy binding twine. The archetypal Norman roof included a clay ridge planted with flowering irises. My father would have loved that – witness his decision to thatch the cottage – but after the First World War, slate had become increasingly popular and the thatched roof had already been replaced. My father had to be content with renovating the deteriorating slates.

Inside, plumbers installed a coal-fired central heating system. It was actually a bit of a stretch to refer to it as central since radiators were installed in just two of the three upstairs rooms and none at ground level.

The downstairs living room had, according to my father, no need for central heating. People had been living in this house for almost four centuries and had managed perfectly well without it. The fireplace was there to be used and not just during the winter months since spring and fall weather can be wickedly unpleasant. My father, who lived to be 80, steadfastly refused to go back on a decision he had made while he was still in his 30s. For him the very soul of his beloved house resided within that ancient open fireplace. He adamantly rejected any suggestion that blocking off its huge flue, even temporarily, might have the beneficial effect of retaining much needed heat within the house. Besides, he loved hauling in three-foot logs from the woodpile in the back garden and setting to work each morning rekindling the fire. Smoke from my father's fires invariably made its way beyond the living room into other parts of the house. The size of the flue was largely to blame – it was wide enough to accommodate a platoon of chimney sweeps – and thus incapable of drawing up the smoke without the presence of a large volume of air. Doors were kept open and we lived in constant draughts. I grew up hating the cold but am, nonetheless, grateful to my father for his reverence for open wood fires. I remember, during winter evenings, watching for hours on end the embers of the fires he had so enthusiastically built in that extraordinarily large hearth. For me it was an intense, dreamy, quasi-mystical experience: a communion of sorts with the countless generations of humans who had preceded me in gathering around such hearths, and this one in particular.

Nor was there any need for radiators in the middle of the three downstairs rooms. The farmers who lived in the house at the time my father purchased it used it as a kitchen and it also had a huge stone fireplace – one of four, two at ground level and two one storey above, that had been built into a single massive stone structure. The flues came together forming a giant chimneystack that rose impressively above the roof.

The business of cooking in an open hearth was a primitive affair. Pots were hung above the embers from chains secured to hooks and frying pans and saucepans were held in place on cast-iron tripods. Most households also had cast-iron spits for roasting meat. Spits, like every other cooking utensil, were placed above whichever part of the open hearth was producing the desired level of heat. Everything in sight was covered in soot.

An innovation that became popular in the mid 1800s was the factory-produced cast iron stove with several cooking rings. When I was the child the neighbours still used such stoves. They were propped up against fireplaces such as the ones in our ancient farmhouse, and their cylindrical iron smoke pipes pushed up inside the centuries old stone chimney flues. The cook was spared the annoyance of smoke and soot but she was responsible for stoking her stove. She depended on a constant supply of dry wood chopped down to size. Charcoal worked best for kindling but it was expensive. I do not know whether my father's farmers had such a stove. My impression is that they had a hard time making ends meet – a 30-acre farm was small even by the standards of the time – so they might have still been cooking on an open hearth. When my parents undertook the renovation of their newly acquired farmhouse, they had to do so without recourse to electricity or gas, and so they opted for a coal-fired cooker. This was a decidedly British innovation. Even back in the 1930s slow burning, constant-heat cooking stoves had become popular in the kitchens of genteel country houses throughout the mist-blanketed British Isles. The Rolls Royce of such stoves was the Aga. Agas were relatively unknown in France but my father had one imported from Sweden at what must have been a huge expense for these behemoths of the cooking world weighed several tons. It was installed in the kitchen, right up against the stonework of the old fireplace and trimmed with tiles.

This modern innovation was not in keeping with the 16th century origins of the farmhouse so I suspect that it was my mother who insisted on this particular luxury. The Aga became one of my mother's most emotionally charged possessions. It was the only genuinely warm place within the entire house. I was brought up with the image of countless English, Scottish, Welsh and Irish families huddling around their Aga while the rest of their gracious homes were given over to unremitting cold and dampness.

It obviously took a while for the farmers to move into the newly built cottage and for the masons, plasterers and roofers to finish renovating the ancient farmhouse. My guess is that by the end of 1938 everything was ready for my parents. Did they in fact move in? Surely not my father since he was still working in London as a journalist. The acquisition of the old farmhouse and its much-needed repairs had severely strained his financial resources so that he needed the money. My parents' lives were about to change in yet another more radical way. By the end of 1938, my mother was in the third month of her pregnancy with me. Doctors advised my parents that since she had already suffered at least one miscarriage, she should rest as much as possible. The suggestion that my mother move to Normandy so she could breathe in unpolluted country air and spend the remaining months of her pregnancy far away from the bustle of London must, at the time, have made a good deal of sense. My father was an experienced traveller and it would be relatively easy for him to make frequent cross Channel sailings via the nearby port of Le Havre.

It is my impression that my mother agreed to this plan only very reluctantly. She loved living in London, enjoyed the many parties to which she and my father were invited – as the writer of a society column for a London evening newspaper he hobnobbed with the rich and famous – and she had come to regard England as her adopted home. There was also another major complication. Her mother also lived in London. She was still a French citizen but after much effort had been granted a residence permit. As mentioned, my French grandmother had not had an easy life. She had lost her second child to meningitis – a two-year old named Robert, had been widowed at an early age and had left Paris for London in the 1920s in the hope of a better life. She had also taken a liking to London and although lacking any schooling beyond elementary grades, had taught herself to read, write and speak English with remarkable fluency. She was a talented dressmaker in an age where society ladies still had their clothes made to measure. So in London she made a living but only just. She, in fact, depended, to an extent, on her son-in-law's generosity – something she resented immensely. The relationships between my grandmother, my father and my mother were fraught with complexity – something that I became very much aware of as I grew up. I could not help taking sides and came to regard my French grandmother as my closest friend and ally.

If, as was feared, my mother was likely to have a difficult pregnancy, she needed more than just rest and fresh air. Would it not be a wonderful idea if her mother were at her side providing her with much needed support? My grandmother was no more inclined to return to France than was my mother but I sense that, in the circumstances, she had little choice but to accept my father's suggestion. That is how my French grandmother became involved in my English father's Norman dream.

From the east-facing window in the largest of the farmhouse's three upstairs rooms there is a good view over the valley and the land rising beyond it. There are distant fields and woodlands and the pleasing silhouette of a 17th century chateau – a reminder that before the Revolution everything within sight was within the fealty of a local *seigneur* who was, in turn, beholden to the King of France. In spite of the building boom of the 1970s and 1980s, this particular view is today much the same as it was at the time of my birth. On clear mornings the sun comes streaming in. It is a cheerful room. My parents had furnished it with a double bed and the plumbers had installed a washbasin with hot and cold water and one of the ancient farmhouse's only three radiators. That was it: no bath, no shower and not even a WC. Those amenities were available downstairs at the other end of the house in a little room off the kitchen that was kept warm in the winter by the presence of a small coal-fired furnace that heated up the hot water for the washbasins and the radiators. My father called it rather grandiosely the boiler room: I imagined us on board a steamship sailing the ocean blue. Should a need arise for really hot water; it had to be brought to a boil in a large, white, enamelled pot placed on the fabled Aga.

My mother was under the care of a local doctor and a midwife. Docteur Lehérissey was a kindly man who in the post war years became a good friend of the family. I remember him well. He was short, slightly bent-over, impeccably dressed in a grey pin-striped suit with matching waistcoat, wore starched white collars, collected stamps and had a charmingly gossipy wife who constantly complained about her good-for-nothing housemaids. He always carried a stethoscope round his neck, and believed, like all good French doctors, in dispensing suppositories and tonics poured out of glass phials. The phials came from the local pharmacy in elaborate cardboard packages that included a small blade for sawing off their necks and releasing their precious contents into a glassful of broth. He also prescribed an inordinate number of injections – something I dreaded – and insisted on everyone's temperature being taken with a huge rectal thermometer.

The midwife kept busy going from farm to farm. In those days it would not have occurred to anyone to go to a hospital to have a baby.

Thus was the setting for my coming into this world in June 1939.

When the much-heralded event actually occurred, my father was not present – he was in London working. By all accounts things did not go at all well. My mother suffered through an excruciatingly long labour – no anaesthetic of any kind was available – and Docteur Lehérissey, assisted by the midwife and my grandmother, had to use forceps to bring me through the breach. My grandmother – used as she was to misfortune – thought at one point her daughter was going to die.

When it was all over, Docteur Lehérissey sat down to write my father a telegram which was taken to the local post office so it could be dispatched to London. How else was my father going to find out about his wife's life threatening delivery and the birth of his son? There was a telephone in the house – telephones then, as now, were not dependent on electrical power – but placing a long-distance call was beyond the capabilities of most people. The idea of calling a foreign country must have been especially daunting. Calls had to be reserved ahead of time, connections were often inaudible and the whole business was expensive beyond belief.

For good measure, Docteur Leherissey also wrote my father a letter and made a point of taking it personally to the post office on his way home. He spoke to the postal clerk sitting behind the caged window to make sure it was correctly stamped. He also told her it was important and so please make it her business to see it went out with the afternoon post. Who knows, the letter might arrive before the telegram.

2

The Wartime Years

The timing of my birth on that June day in 1939 was somewhat unfortunate. Following Hitler's invasion of Poland in September, Britain and France declared war on Germany. Despite the declaration of war, my mother remained in Normandy with her newborn and my father continued to commute intermittently from London for long weekends. Britain deployed troops in France but neither Germany nor the allies launched direct attacks on each other. Suddenly, shortly before my first birthday, the so-called phony phase of the war came abruptly to an end and the situation became hugely threatening. On May 10, 1940, Winston Churchill replaced Neville Chamberlain as British prime minister and Germany invaded the Netherlands, Belgium and France. Within weeks, the German army had made a mockery of the French defences by outflanking the Maginot Line, Belgium had collapsed and panic ensued. The French population took to the highways in a futile attempt to escape the invading German army and the whole of Europe fell apart.

My father - although he was a journalist with access to newsrooms - was, like almost everyone else, taken completely by surprise by the swiftness of France's collapse. During those fateful days in May of 1940 he and my mother found themselves on opposite shores of the English Channel: he working in his London newspaper office and the rest of his family in the ancient farmhouse. The situation soon turned desperate; the British had their hands full evacuating their expeditionary force from Dunkirk and refugees now overwhelmed many of France's main roads. My father suddenly realised he had made a grievous mistake by waiting in London as long as he had. He now needed to find a way to cross over to France, rescue his family and somehow find a way back to England. As a British journalist, he could expect nothing but trouble from the invading German forces. Regular cross

Channel sailings linking London and Paris had been discontinued and only by luck did he succeed in securing a passage on a ship bound for Saint Malo: a port in Brittany considerably to the west of Paris, and likely to remain beyond the reach of the German army for at least a little longer. Once in Saint Malo he still faced the challenge of making his way to the Normandy coast beyond the city of Caen - a difficult journey of over 100 miles - and hope that my mother would still be waiting for him. What if she had given up hope and joined the stream of refugees going west? They had no way of communicating with each other.

Fortunately, my father made it back to the farmhouse and my mother was still waiting for him. It was now clearer than ever that the French government was on the verge of collapse and that the Germans were about to enter Paris. My father realised that the only possible escape route was to retrace his steps west to the port of Saint Malo in the hope that ships might still be sailing to England. My parents did not own a car and trains and buses had stopped running. Fortunately, a friend with a car and with a few spare gallons of petrol offered to take my father, my mother, my grandmother and me, the baby, half the distance to Saint Malo. From there they would have to rely on sheer luck and hopefully find someone willing to help them continue the journey west. Fortunately, my father had had the foresight to bring enough cash to pay the exorbitant fare that would surely be demanded of him.

There was indeed a British ship in Saint Malo; probably one of the very last to sail out ahead of the arrival of the German army. My mother had acquired a British passport on marrying my father so that she, my British-born father and I as their child - notwithstanding my French birth - were allowed on board. Not so my grandmother for she was French. The fact that she had taken up residence in London as far back as the 1920s apparently counted for nothing. For her, naturalisation as a British subject must have been an unattainable goal. One of the harsh consequences of her agreeing to return to France - the Normandy of my father's dreams - so she could care for my mother and her newborn, had been the loss of her legal right to reside in Britain.

Only much later in life did I begin to reflect on the enormity of the consequences of that parting in faraway Saint Malo. My French grandmother had virtually no family and she had nowhere to go. Returning to the Normandy farmhouse was out of the question. The farmers who had been resettled in the cottage had turned out to be a querulous, unscrupulous bunch and for them the onset of war was a heaven-sent opportunity to move back into the farmhouse from which they had been dislodged.

My grandmother was not a particularly gregarious person and the few friends she had made were still in London where she had lived for the past 20 years. She had no money. My father must have emptied his pockets giving her whatever he still had – not much considering the small fortune the driver with petrol to spare must have charged him for agreeing to make the last leg of the trip to Saint Malo. I imagine her holding me during that long journey over roads crowded with refugees, feeding me, changing my nappies, and smothering me with kisses – for I later learned that that is what grandmothers are wont to do – and then having to hand me back to my mother as the ship was about to set sail.

My mother would have to wait for the liberation of Paris in September 1944 – four whole years later – to resume meaningful contact with my grandmother. She had indeed survived the war. From Saint Malo, she had made her way back to Paris. She had one remaining relative living there: a kindly man by the name of Louis who had married her sister Marie-Thérèse. He was a widower. Marie-Thérèse, a tragic figure, had died after a long struggle with cancer leaving an only child, a daughter, Rolande, who had also died: not of cancer but of tuberculosis. That had been another long struggle. Rolande, the cousin I would never know, had died just after the declaration of war.

I was brought up listening to my mother's telling and retelling of these stories. She was quite practised in the evocation of doom.

Thanks to Louis' kindness my grandmother found not only a place to stay but also a job to support herself – barely – working, once again, as a seamstress. Extraordinary as it may seem by the standards of our contemporary world, there was simply no means by which my mother and grandmother could have been in regular contact with each other. Cross-Channel mail and telephone service had come to an abrupt halt with the German invasion of France and the risks involved in attempting to communicate through networks of underground resistance operatives were unacceptably high. Only thanks to the International Red Cross were messages eventually exchanged.

When my father and mother, babe in arms, disembarked in Southampton, they were broke. My father had spent all he had ever saved on the farm in Normandy and the war had done away with his job. Newspapers were no longer running society columns. He found work, though, eventually settling for a war-related job with a government ministry dealing with some kind of propaganda effort. My parents found a flat in London. The best thing about it was the address in Hartford Street, Mayfair – by Shepherd Market and within an easy walk of Green Park. Since central London was an obvious target for the German Luftwaffe, the rent was cheap – probably a lot cheaper than many other far less prestigious addresses.

My father's way of dealing with adversity was to sharpen his pen. With good reason because when it came to writing, he was a master craftsman. He had fallen in love with writing at an early age and could not have conceived of earning a living any other way. His mother's inherited wealth not only provided him with a French governess, it also gave him the opportunity to go to Eton. He spoke of his old school with great affection especially, it seems, because rather than being forced to play team sports, he had been left alone there to pursue his love of books. His father had wanted him to go on to Oxford so he could prepare himself for an honourable profession such as the Church or medicine but that was not what my father had in mind. Instead, much to his father's chagrin, he immediately embarked on a career in journalism, indulging his love of travel and making use of his fluency in French. His decision to marry a penniless, French, working-class girl in her early 20s – pretty as she was – only increased his family's disappointment. It set my father on a highly independent course and caused him to rely on his pen as a means of surviving. Interviewing some of the leading politicians of his time and writing society columns was a way of generating much needed cash but my father's real ambition was to become a published author. He had, in fact published a book before the war. It was a quite scholarly account of the lives of some of the more interesting members of his mother's family. It was the story of how his great-grandmother, the daughter of one of the founders of the Rothschild banking fortune had married into a politically prominent English aristocratic family.

The advent of war, combined with what had turned out to be a disastrously timed investment in his Normandy farmhouse, had robbed my father of his entire material wealth. He could have asked his mother to help him out either with a loan or even with an outright cash gift. She was a generously inclined person and although the small portion of the fortune that had come down to her from her Rothschild parentage had shrunk, there still remained more than enough to allow her and her now retired clergyman husband to live comfortably in a country house in Guildford, not far from London. My father could even have reasoned that he was owed something, given the fact that his two sisters, neither of whom had married, depended on family patronage for their own genteel way of life. To ask his mother for such a favour would, however, have gone against my father's fiercely independent streak. Instead, he turned to his pen, not just in the hope of making some of the extra money he sorely needed to supplement his meagre salary as a writer of wartime government-issued propaganda, but to get even with the dismal hand fate had dealt him.

In this, and in other ways, my father was actually quite lucky. He regarded himself as being the most unmilitary of men and he avoided being conscripted. It was his second narrow escape. The years he had spent at Eton reading poetry and studying the classics had also been the years of the First World War. The huge shadow cast by the Great War must have reinforced his feeling that the fates, by allowing him to lead this idyllic even if strictly temporary existence, had magnanimously granted him a reprieve from the grimness to which everyone else in his generation had been condemned. He had fully expected to be drafted on his 18th birthday but the 1918 Armistice had come just in time. This time around he was 39 when hostilities broke out and disaster struck at Dunkirk. He was therefore at an age where it was relatively easy for a man to argue that he could better serve the war effort by remaining a civilian. Thanks to his official job, my father once again avoided military conscription. Perhaps living in Mayfair and serving as a fire watchman several nights a week was dangerous enough. The closest he ever came to military service was stalking the blacked-out streets of London with a torch at the ready, wearing a blue uniform and a fireman's helmet.

My father found his job at the propaganda ministry – I'm not sure exactly which government department he worked for, but that is what he called it – boring in the extreme. There were, however, in addition to the subsistence wages he brought home, several good things about it. First of all the offices of this particular ministry were in Whitehall and he was in the habit of going there on foot, walking across St. James's Park in plain view of Buckingham Palace. It was not the safest route on the days the Germans were on a bombing spree but he loved the walk. He would sometimes take me with him. There were ducks on the pond – even in wartime – with old ladies feeding them crusts, even though bread was rationed. Love of walking is one of my father's gifts to me. The second thing is that he bought home paper clips, scissors, coloured index cards and pots of glue. Not an authorised use of government property, I'm sure, but objects that for me were a source of wonderment; a means of tiptoeing into a fantasy world that was mine and mine only. By far the most important perk, however, was time. It was a job that taxed my father so little that it left him with time and energy to do what he really wanted to do which, of course, was to write.

My father was, to his chagrin, no novelist. He could only write well about things he had experienced. What better source material than the saga of the ancient Normandy farmhouse? It was in a sense a war story and therefore had plenty of dramatic elements. It was a small piece of paradise lost. The object of my father's quest now lay in an impenetrable never-never land cut off from the rest of the world. I also sense that my father felt that the fates owed him some small return on his investment; a consolation dividend paid out on what would otherwise have been a disastrous piece of business. Besides the loss was not just financial, it was also emotional. I would learn much later in my own life that writing is one of the best therapies for dealing with loss. So my father set to work writing up the saga. He needed help though. The acquisition of the farmhouse might have been his dream but in the end my mother had spent much more time there than he had. It was she who had shopped in the village, gossiped with the cleaning ladies, listened to the neighbours' life stories, talked to the tenant farmers and visited the surrounding farms. My mother, it turned out, had a natural gift for storytelling. She had an excellent memory, knew how to pick up the essentials of a story and then embroider it just enough to spice it up in the retelling. Having experienced poverty and struggled to survive at an early age, she was not inclined to sugarcoat her stories. She could be very funny but was, above all, devastatingly perceptive when it came to exposing human weakness. There were no holds barred – I don't remember my mother ever worrying too much about how someone might feel on recognising themselves in one of the characters she wrote about.

I imagine that at the beginning my father listened to what she had to say and then did the actual writing. He, after all, was the writer. She had received little schooling beyond the elementary grades and hardly any of that had been in English. But then, at some point, a more cooperative pattern began to emerge. My mother had mastered the French language in her own way – not the language of academicians but the language of storytellers. She wrote quickly and with extraordinary accuracy. She was a natural speller and had a flair for the grammatical rules that are so often the undoing of the French. My father soon realised that it was much better to have her do her own writing. He would then take her handwritten manuscripts, translate them into English and, typing away at his Smith Corona, incorporate them into his own story about the farm in Normandy. That became the title of the book:

A Farm in Normandy. My father had little difficulty finding a publisher and the book came out in 1941 under his own name. My parents had not even thought it necessary to disguise the names of the people appearing in my mother's stories. Why bother? This was 1941 and the chances of anyone surviving the war to sue my parents for defamation of character did not, at the time, seem very high. Besides my mother had written the truth about all these people: too bad if they didn't find it flattering. The book sold well: in those days the sellout of a first edition running into several thousand copies was considered something of a coup. I doubt it made much difference to the family budget but it must have lifted my parents' morale no end.

Then my father started writing about what it was like living in Mayfair in the middle of a war with a young child and a dog - my mother's snub-nosed, longhaired tan Pekingese that went by the very French and very onomatopoeic name of Pouffy. Of course my mother added her own stories to the mix. They had hit upon a viable literary formula. I was at that time still blissfully unaware of what it was like to live with people who were hell-bent on turning anything they could lay their hands on - however insignificant and personal - into a publishable story.

The Mayfair flat with the bargain rent was on the ground floor and consisted of only two rooms, both overlooking an inner courtyard. The entire family slept in one of them. My cot was against the wall by the door and most of the remaining space was taken up by my parents' double bed. The other room was chockablock with furniture: my father's plain white, wood desk at which he sat endlessly tapping away on one of his typewriters, an oval polished mahogany table covered in knickknacks and a narrow settee upholstered in yellow shiny silk propped against the wall. The yellow settee was for guests only. I had no rights over any of these precious objects although I was in fact allowed to crawl over the floor so long as I did so quietly - especially when my father was working. My mother presided over the kitchen. It was a small, windowless, austere room, lit by a single light bulb. It had a refrigerator, a gas stove, a sink and just about enough space for a square table around which all the good things of life - meals in particular - seemed to revolve. Fortunately there was an entrance hall - windowless, of course, but large enough to store my pram - and later, when I became conscious of them, my books together with a tiny desk on which I could scribble to my heart's content. This was the one place that was particularly my own and from which parental supervision was largely absent.

I have great difficulty sorting my early childhood memories. Some are of events I undoubtedly experienced myself while I suspect others of being layered into my consciousness from listening to oft-repeated stories. I can conjure up an image of what my first year on this earth might have been like. I am being held in my grandmother's arms in front of the ancient farmhouse's half-timbered façade, breathing in the good Normandy air and listening to the lowing cows in the field below. Pure imagination! I do, however, have what seems to be a very early memory and is certainly a very vivid one. I am standing with my father on a wide street not far from Green Park and I am watching a large building collapse. Clouds of dust are emerging from the rubble and sirens are sounding. I am not particularly frightened, since I am holding my father's hand and I am vaguely aware that it is normal for things like this to occur. This could, of course, be a composite memory. Several years later, after the Battle of Britain, the Germans, in a last desperate attempt to win the war, were again pounding London with bombs, but this time delivering them with their technologically superior rockets, the V1 doodlebugs. They would whir overhead and then, just after falling silent, visit destruction on whatever happened to be in their way. I was much older then so I remember all that quite clearly but I also remember being frightened. This was real fear, the kind of fear that can no longer be dismissed with a mother's kiss or a father's firm hand. In that other memory of earlier destruction fear is absent.

I do remember sirens: haunting sounds associated with bombs falling from the sky. In the bowels of the earth below the London flat – *le flat*, as my French mother called it – were box rooms. So-called not because they were box shaped which they indeed were, but because they were there to store boxes; hat boxes, boxes full of books and, of course, the cabin trunks of those who in happier days went on cruises or travelled to far away parts of the Empire such as India. When the sirens sounded, the flats had to be evacuated and most of the time we made our way down to the box rooms. Down, down we went. Box rooms were strange places with naked light bulbs dangling from wires and grey, rough, breeze blocks. What I remember most was the smell. The adjective dank hardly does it justice; it was the complex, hard-to-describe smell of raw concrete, dusty, humid and persistent. I have other memories of going down into London Underground stations in the middle of the night, clutching Thermos flasks of hot tea and blankets and lying down on the platform. I just do not think they are quite as real. These are stories I had heard over and over again. They were part of living in London during the war and perhaps I just assumed that I also had been part of them. The box room memories are of another kind. They bear the seal of genuineness for I was the only one who could have experienced the smell that accompanied them.

Then I formed fleeting images of guests welcomed into the flat - of cups of coffee drunk in the little kitchen and even meals served on the mahogany table temporarily cleared of its clutter. Everyone spoke French. Much later, it was explained to me that the visitors were members of General De Gaulle's London staff, and that many of these men and women were risking their lives by being parachuted into German occupied France to help organise the growing Resistance movement. My mother, of course, hoped against hope that one day one of them would come back with news of my grandmother.

I have other more prosaic memories. The bewilderment of my parents confronted with my childhood temper tantrums and my feeling of injustice and resentment as they vainly and misguidedly tried to calm me down with repeated slapping and scolding. There I was standing beside the mahogany table next to the window looking out on the courtyard, holding on desperately to a yellow coat which for some reason my mother had decided I should take off, screeching, tears pouring down my face, quite convinced that I was the unhappiest child in the world and my parents monstrous people. The memory is fixed to the exact spot on which I was standing or, more precisely, stomping and yelling. Then there was my fascination with looking out of the bedroom window into the courtyard, watching taxis and cars coming to the front door of the building. As the years passed I became able to tell a Morris apart from an Austin and a Rolls Royce from a Bentley. The flat is like a memory palace with distant images linked to the different parts of each room but I have no sense of the timing of these events, understandably so because my parents, creatures of habit, lived in it far beyond the war years.

With the war over and me moving out of infancy into childhood, the flat became far too small for the three of us. It ceased to be home for me and, quite naturally, I looked elsewhere to find space for my growing emotional roots.

3

Childhood In Normandy

I remember the end of the war – or at least the end of the war in Europe in May 1945. I had never heard so much noise and seen so many people in the streets. There were crowds in Piccadilly Circus and in Leicester Square and people were everywhere, shouting, climbing lamp posts, waving flags and downing pints of beer. Apart from being intimidated, I do not remember much else – except that at some point after that my father was given permission to return to France: not my mother, though, because it was felt that travelling through war-torn Europe was just too dangerous for women. He managed to return to the farm and there found my grandmother who, in the aftermath of the German retreat and against considerable odds, had found a way of returning to Normandy. So my grandmother was safe and the ancient house, although looted by the tenant farmers, had withstood the German occupation.

I knew about my grandmother because my mother talked about her all the time. For as long as I could remember, my mother had made me say my prayers at the foot of my bed last thing at night and always, always, mention was made of my grandmother in France. We did not pray as much for my English grandmother Euphemia. There was obviously far less need to, because every month or so we went by train to see her for lunch on a Sunday in Guildford. She had long white hair and I do not remember saying a lot to her. Having to speak English probably made me shy. What I do remember is the garden around her house because, living in a London flat, it was the only garden I ever had a chance to play in. It was full of flowers and quite unlike Green Park on the other side of Piccadilly from our Mayfair flat and where my mother took me for daily walks, together with Pouffy. I also remember walking through the fields on the way to my English grandmother's house from the station and my parents being yelled at by a farmer who objected to our walking over his sugar beets – those things I do remember. But obviously, it was my French grandmother who needed the prayers.

A little later it was my mother's turn to make the journey to France. She took a large suitcase full of food with her for my grandmother who, according to my parents, had suffered through the war years without so much as a single decent meal. I remember that when my mother came back she had a gift for me – a small see-through toy-like house with a pretty red roof and a little chimney. My mother told me there were no longer any real toys in France – the Germans had seen to that – and that the little house was used to collect food stamps in restaurants. If people did not slip stamps through the roof into the little house they were not allowed to eat. The Germans were gone, but all this mess was of their making. That much I understood. Even in London, my mother had spent the war years bartering food stamps for cigarette coupons, and she knew just how much to tip butchers especially when it came to calves brains and other good things such as tripe that the English were not in the habit of eating. All those stamps and coupons looked pretty drab to me; the French could at least be thankful for those pretty little houses.

I have no way of telling when it was that my mother finally took me back to my native Normandy: probably some time in 1946 when things had settled down enough to allow unrestricted civilian travel across the English Channel. That is when I became conscious of meeting my French grandmother for the first time. I know she had seen me at the very moment of my birth but this was quite different. I must, after all, have been approaching my seventh birthday. Quite unlike my English grandmother she had short red hair and lots of freckles. My mother and I must have travelled via Paris and therefore taken the train to Deauville from the Gare Saint Lazare. She met us at the station. I was terribly intimidated and instead of using the familiar 'tu', used the formal 'vous'. She was crestfallen, but it did not last. We were to become the best of friends.

The farmhouse with the ancient timbers in which I had taken my first breath seven years earlier was still standing but it had been looted. The walls were bare, the furniture gone and even the famous Aga cooker, heavy as it was, had been pried out, hoisted into a horse-drawn tumbrel and removed. The cottage had also been ransacked. The removal of the Aga was attributed to the local German commandant who had requisitioned it for personal use. As for the looting of everything else, my parents had reason to suspect the locals. Why not after all? Had not my parents gone for good? Besides, there were several right-minded Vichy government sympathisers in the neighbourhood who would have had no qualms dispossessing my parents for patriotic reasons. There were some among Maréchal Pétain's supporters who during the war years had thought of the English, rather than the Germans, as France's traditional enemies.

When it was all over my parents got their Aga back and a grandfather clock but not much else. It was a miserable time during which the French had little choice but to come to terms with the humiliations endured during the German occupation and with the meanness and treacheries brought about by the fear it had spawned. In London, my parents had met Resistance heroes, many of whom after being parachuted back into occupied territory had been hunted down by the Gestapo and died for their ideals. This was the other side of the coin. My mother considered England to be her adopted country and had found happiness there but she remained fiercely French. These were, indeed, painful and humiliating times.

The tenant farmers for whom my parents had built the cottage had also gone. For my parents, that was just as well. There was, however, a grim and tragic story underlying their disappearance. The farmer and his wife were often at odds with each other, and he had taken to regularly beating her into submission. Her father lived a few villages away and, in collusion with the farmer's eldest son, devised a devilish plan to take revenge on his son-in-law. The farmer, in defiance of the rules imposed by the German occupying army, had hidden his hunting gun under a floorboard in the old cider press at the bottom of our field. The son, knowing exactly where the gun was hidden, was persuaded by the old man to inform the Germans of its whereabouts. The Germans lost no time and had the father arrested that very evening. He was immediately deported to a German labour camp and never seen again. After the war, the French authorities came to arrest the old man but he slit his own throat before the gendarmes could grab him. As for the son, he was tried and found guilty of treason. The rest of the family fell apart and my parents never rented the cottage again.

My grandmother's forced exile in Paris during the war had been very difficult. Her work as a seamstress brought in barely enough to make ends meet. There simply was not enough work to go around in German-occupied Paris. The Vichy government had in fact organised a network of social services for the destitute and, under the auspices of one of Maréchal Pétain's programmes, she was eventually given a salaried position making winter blankets by sewing together patches cut out of discarded clothes. The job included a free midday meal and it turned out to be a lifesaver. There was, after all, some good to the Vichy government.

When in 1946 I was reunited with my grandmother, she had just crossed the threshold into her 60s. My sense is that she felt old for her age, weighed down by the many difficulties that had come her way. Nothing had come easily to her. Only 18 when my mother was born out of wedlock, she was penniless and very lonely. She did marry several years later – by all accounts she was an exceptionally attractive redhead – and her young husband took the legal step of recognising my mother as his child. I don't think it was a particularly happy marriage – my grandfather was a humble man who treated my mother with kindness but he was also prone to flying into terrible tempers and in time he took to drink. While still in his 40s he died of pneumonia. All that was bad enough for my grandmother but it was as nothing compared with the loss of her two-year-old son, who died of a virulent form of meningitis in a dingy Paris hospital. This little boy, who would have been my uncle, and I were given the same name. Robert was, of course, my father's name but, as far as my grandmother was concerned, it was the name she had given her beloved son. I was too young to be told about those tragedies, let alone understand the devastating impact they had had on my beloved grandmother, but what she could talk to me about was the sadness she had experienced that August afternoon in 1940 in Saint Malo when she had been forced to hand me back to my mother and face her own lonely exile in Paris.

My mother and my grandmother were indissolubly bonded together by the circumstances of their lives, and I have no doubt that they loved each other intensely, but they quarrelled and fought ferociously. My mother must have suffered from huge pangs of guilt. I always took my grandmother's side. How could I not? She took mine consistently – we were natural allies against all that was unfair in the world.

The relationship between my father and my grandmother was distant and yet fraught with complexity. How could it be otherwise? She was wholly dependent on his financial support – an awkward situation for a proud person to be in, particularly since it entailed a number of offsetting obligations. My father had never given up working in London. His propaganda job had naturally petered out with the end of the war and so he was back in business as a journalist. When my parents were in London my grandmother stepped into the role of de facto caretaker at the farmhouse in Normandy. The mere thought that this made her into some kind of servant must have been abhorrent to her. My mother was, of course, right in the middle of all this and there were fireworks aplenty. Tempers often flared between my mother and my grandmother and my parents were among themselves practiced quarrellers. I had become used to these grand shows and assumed that this was how all families operated. I was hardly in a position to make comparisons.

While in London I had never had the opportunity to make any friends of my age. Many children had been evacuated out of the city into the countryside on the theory that they would be less vulnerable to German bombings. Besides, I was never sent to school. My father made no bones about the fact that he didn't believe in them. I think his aversion to schooling was somehow connected with the idea that schools rob parents of their ability to influence their children. He had certainly succeeded in winning my mother over to this idea. I was, of course, far too young to be aware of any of this at the time but I can now see that my parents' decision to keep me out of school for as long as they possibly could had a lot to do with their desire to mould me into an ideal that was of their making. I have no doubt that many parents harbour such illusions but my perception is that mine had a particularly bad case of this particular affliction. The fact that I was an only child must have been an exacerbating factor.

Thus it was that I was taught at home, and I cannot say that I have fond memories of my parents' efforts to teach me. Learning to read does not seem to have gone too badly and, so far as I can tell, I acquired that particular skill almost effortlessly. Learning to write was another matter. I remember sitting at the polished oval table in the flat in London, propped up on cushions stacked on a chair, a blank sheet of paper before me on which my father had drawn straight lines with a pencil. I was being told to write into the spaces between the lines the letters 'b' and 'p' and all I could do was cry loudly and shed large tears all over the paper. I can still picture my father, obviously equally upset and indignant, standing over me, a bath towel tied around his waist, upbraiding me with repeated warnings that I was well on my way to becoming a total failure and that it was common knowledge that at my age Winston Churchill was already capable of writing effortlessly. The more I cried the worse it felt. I remember similar sessions with my mother, although those particular memories are probably from later years. She was making me do dictations and I was confusing all those ghastly word endings that in French all sound the same but can be adjectives or participles or infinitives depending on the way they are spelt. I was muddling up all those horrible words with double consonants and mute syllables that can be either 'a' or 'e' and not caring a whit about it all, struggling with the unhappy reality that life could be utterly miserable. How come my grandmother never put me though this kind of torture but my parents did?

The multiplication tables were just as painful. According to my parents, a child who could not master his multiplication tables would grow up to be perfectly useless, incapable of holding down any kind of job. "They wouldn't even take you at the Post Office," my mother would say, scornfully. I knew about the village post office in Normandy. It was built of faux 1930s half-timbering, had a decorative façade with fussy little roofs that reminded me of an outsize cuckoo clock and inside it everything reeked of smoke from nasty little yellow cigars and Gauloises cigarettes. Even the customers, who had to stand in line, reeked of smoke. I had a fond spot for the post office, particularly since it was just across the street from the smithy where, given half a chance, I would spend hours looking at huge carthorses being shod. I loved the smell of burning hoof and the shushing sound when the smith dipped red-hot horseshoes into a bucket full of water. I did not quite see what the post office had to do with my problems with multiplication tables.

"Had I given any thought to what I wanted to do with my life?" my mother would exclaim. "Obviously not," she would add in the same breath, but it was high time I did. How come I could never remember six times seven? "Forty-two!" I remember my mother yelling out at me. "That'll be my age next year. I can't bear the idea. You don't realise how terrible it is to be forty-two. Even now, when I look at myself in the mirror, I realise that I'm already an old woman. I'll soon be dead and then you'll be sorry you didn't pay more attention to your old mother. My hair will soon be turning white." I must have been eight at the time but this is just one memory among many. My impression is that French dictations and stormy efforts to teach me multiplication tables punctuated a good many of my childhood years. As to my mother's lament, I have photographs of her in her early 40s. She had rich, silky long hair, a smooth skin and an attractively proportioned round face – she was an exceptionally good-looking woman. She had not even reached the mid-point of her life span.

My father was also an enthusiastic proponent of the educational virtues of the multiplication table, but his fondest goal was to do everything in his power to turn me into a journalist. He showed himself, at least in the pursuit of this particular goal, somewhat gentler. I remember a winter spent in Normandy. Both my parents were there, so my father must for some reason have been out of a job. There was nothing terribly unusual about that. His independent ways often irritated newspaper editors so he was used to getting what he referred to as 'the sack'. Besides, the literary arrangement he and my mother had chanced upon was turning out better than expected, so he must have welcomed the extra time. I know that he had loved that winter spent in the ancient farmhouse because it was something he talked about in later years. When he was not in the upstairs room at the far end of the narrow corridor at the top of the staircase – the room with the three-feet thick stonewalls – working on his Smith Corona, he was outside chopping up dead apple trees.

The living room with the huge fireplace was the focus of his activity. We were expected to spend our evenings around the hearth. He built large fires each evening that burnt into the night, eventually leaving a bed of smouldering embers. My father liked reading aloud. The book he had chosen that winter was *Middlemarch* by George Eliot. He had a thing about women authors and he believed that the way to master a language was to read its classics aloud. Most of this, I now realise, was for my benefit – for the furtherance of my education. I cannot say that I remember very much about George Eliot's great novel but these were indeed happy times. This was, at long last, learning English without tears. When the nights were cold we would wrap ourselves up in warm blankets to guard against the draught escaping up the huge chimney flue. The enchantment came from gazing into the embers and watching flames dart back and forth between the remnants of the large logs my father had brought in from the fields earlier in the day. I was also already very much aware of the antiquity of the house. I knew that the year 1555 was etched into the small marble tile set into the stonework of the fireplace. My father, as a great lover of books, had told me that this was just a few years before Shakespeare's birth and that Elizabeth I would soon become Queen of England. It was, according to him, an amazingly exciting time to have lived because only a century had passed since Gutenberg had printed his first bible and that by then poets and writers all over Europe were busy publishing their works. Even though I was far too young to have an appreciation of what all that meant, I could see that it was immensely important to my father.

Each morning, after breakfast, my father would make it his business to clear the fireplace of grey wood ash, and bring in kindling and a fresh supply of logs for the new day. He then went around the room with duster and broom. After he had dealt with the large table facing the fireplace, I was expected to sit at it and open up a bound exercise book with black covers. Meanwhile my mother was out of the way, upstairs, sitting up in bed, writing. Whatever she produced would then be handed over to my father who then spent most of the afternoon shut up in his room tapping away at his typewriter. Only later would I understand what all this was about. My own writing assignment consisted of filling two fresh pages with handwriting: and not just any old handwriting. It had to be an account of what I had done the day before – in English, no less. I had a nib pen, the kind that had to be dipped into an inkwell and then left enormous and enduring stain marks on most of the fingers of my right hand. "Well, come on now," my father would say encouragingly, "just write about what you did yesterday. It doesn't have to be anything extraordinary. What you think is unimportant becomes interesting when you write it down for other people to read. That is what writers do. Fifty years from now people will want to know what you did yesterday." I would squirm and fidget in the throes of early-onset writer's block. "You had better get on with it," warned my father, mop in hand, "because otherwise you will have to spend all day chewing the end of your pen and then you won't have anything to write about tomorrow. That could be a problem."

The fact is that compared to living in a two room flat in Mayfair, this place was heaven – even if my mother did go on and on with her French dictations and multiplication tables. My essays – that is how my father referred to my daily writing assignment – were no doubt quite repetitive, but they did reflect the enchantment of living in this funny old house half way down a field full of milking cows and bent-over apple trees. Much of my stories revolved around my grandmother. My day had a routine. My first job was to go and fetch the milk from the nearby farm. We had no refrigerator, so this was a daily task. I walked down the field to the stream by the cider press, sloshed across it in my black wellingtons, and then up again through a field that did not belong to us, through a gate across a country lane and then to the farm. The farmer kept a couple of carthorses in that second field and, on the days they were not out working, they often waited expectantly by the gate. These horses were huge. They had never done anyone the slightest harm but they terrified me. I loved the farm, the heavy smell of the milk in the dairy, the heifers crowding around the duck pond, the farmer's wife stoking her kitchen stove and the chickens forever scratching around for grubs. I would write about the menacing horses, embroidering as best I could, filling up as many lines as I could reasonably get away with.

I was also responsible for the cider the family drank at lunchtime. Since my grandmother was the cook and I hung around her as much as possible, I would look to her for a sign that it was time for me to run down to the cider press. So back I would go down the field toward the stream. Today I feel nostalgic thinking about the press. It was a large, thatched barn with the press at the centre. Here the farmer made his cider each autumn after the apples had been gathered in. The apples were first placed for crushing inside a large circular stone trough. A carthorse went round and round, pulling along with it a pair of massive wooden wheels that turned inside the trough crushing the apples into a soft mush. The fruity sweet-smelling mush was then gathered into burlap sacks for stacking within a frame placed under a beam hewn out of the trunk of a giant oak tree. The juice was pressed out of the mush by the sheer weight of the beam as it was gradually lowered. The part of the cider making process that really amazed me, when I first saw it as a child and that has remained etched in my memory, is how the beam was lowered. The beam was threaded to a giant screw which, incredibly, was hand carved from the trunk of yet another oak. A couple of men provided the muscle power required to turn the screw. They did so by pushing each end of a long pole threaded at the base of the massive wooden screw. This is the way Normans had pressed their apples into cider over the centuries. It could be that the cider press was as old as our farmhouse: perhaps even older, there was no way of knowing.

The cider was kept in large oak casks stored in an above ground cellar that was beside the press. My job was to borrow the key to the cellar - it hung from a special hook next to the kitchen sink - ask my grandmother for a pitcher, run down to the press, unlock the cellar - it had a huge wooden door with ancient cast iron hinges - fill the pitcher from the spigot at the bottom of one of the oak casks that seemed almost as tall as the carthorses in the next-door field and rush back up the hill with the pitcher three-quarters full in time for lunch. This is not a job I was particularly good at. In my hurry, I frequently tripped up against a clod, a cowpat, or caught my boot in a hole. Norman fields are no lawns. That made for spilled cider and even broken pitchers. My mother would get after me with the usual recriminations: had I forgotten that pitchers cost money and that making ends meet was hard enough as it was? I could deal with spilled and even broken pitchers. What was far worse was losing the key to the cellar. It was a huge old-fashioned cylindrically shaped key with honest-to-goodness indentations. My grandmother had even drilled a hole into a large piece of wood and secured the key to it with a piece of red twine so it could be seen from a considerable distance. I still managed to lose it surprisingly often. "Oh no, not again," my parents would intone in chorus. "Well you are not sitting down to lunch until you find it. What have we done to deserve such a child?" Sobbing, and also putting on a grand old show of my own, I would walk up and down the path to the cider press ostensibly looking for it until it magically reappeared – generally thanks to my grandmother who could be relied on to figure out where I might have left it: at the edge of the sink to which I had been sent to wash my hands, or beside one of the cats whose presence had distracted me from my appointed task. It was as if some troublemaker of a magician had cast a spell over the cider press key: a spell that only my grandmother could undo.

I remember summer haymaking as a time of particular magic. In rural France in the late 1940s and early 1950s tractors were still beyond the means of small farmers, so that old man Déliquaire, whose cows grazed my father's land, still relied to a considerable extent on horsepower for tasks such as haymaking. The hay was cut with a horse-drawn cutting bar. The bar itself was a tricky piece of equipment powered by a two-stroke hand-cranked petrol engine that required a lot of coaxing. The bane of Norman haymakers was having enough sun to dry the hay sufficiently before bailing it. Drying required turning the hay before gathering it in, something that was often accomplished by running a giant, horse-drawn rake over the cut hay field. Bailing was a particularly demanding physical task. The farmers liked to have their hay bailed, though. It withstood humidity better and was easier to take down from haylofts for feeding to over wintering cows. The bailer was a tough, brawny, highly skilled operator who often hired himself out by the day. He made his own twine out of twisted hay and then used it to bind into shape the bales he had made by kneeling over large, bent bundles of dry hay. The old hand-bound bales were square and extraordinarily tight but not so heavy that a strong man couldn't pitch them into a horse-drawn hay cart and thence into a barn loft.

I loved being with the haymakers. The breaks for a snack of large chunks of bread and wedges of Camembert cheese were times of particular delight. The men drank coffee out of pitchers prepared by the womenfolk. It was thick, dark coffee, and mixed into it were generous amounts of recently distilled, high-alcohol-content Calvados. Some pick me up! I was allowed to smell it and once in a while suck a lump of sugar that had been dipped into this deliciously forbidden mixture. Perhaps the best of all was to be allowed to ride at the top of the hay carts, filled as they were to capacity with bales and loose hay. Each cart was drawn by two horses and moved slowly along the rutted hedge-lined lanes. I remember lying on my back gazing up into the sky as low-lying branches from the oaks, wild cherry trees and hazelnut bushes brushed over me. On a warm July evening when the sun was still high in the sky this was indeed a foretaste of heaven. I would rush home, tell my grandmother about the day's adventures, secure in the knowledge that the next morning I would have plenty to write about.

It is true that my grandmother hankered after her pre-war life in London and made much of lamenting the events that had brought it to an end – not least her daughter marrying this rather eccentric Englishman who by some unhappy chance had also fallen in love with Normandy – but at the same time she really did have an affinity for the countryside. There was something of the peasant in her. It was a quality that I came to recognise as being very much part of the French soul and it was through her that I came to inherit a little piece of it. She had her patch of kitchen garden thanks to which I came to learn how peas, beans, salads and radishes come into this world and why slugs, bugs and beetles of all kinds had to be kept at bay. Then she had her chickens and her rabbits. She raised her chickens the old fashioned way by feeding them scraps from the table, and holding back sufficient eggs so she could have a broody hen sit over them for a full 21 days. She would detail me off so I could vouch for the fact that the rooster was paying appropriate attention to the hens: otherwise, she assured me, the eggs would be useless. There were ample opportunities for me to corroborate this particularly intriguing piece of information, such as when the farmers led their cow to the neighbour's bull and I sneaked away from home so I could accompany them and witness the event. It was quite a performance but, according to my grandmother, fundamentally no different from what our own chickens did at home. We could take pride in that; there was nothing wrong with our chickens. Nor with my grandmother's rabbits for that matter. I know I could never have had these kinds of conversations with my parents so there were limits to what I could report in the daily two-page 'essays' I composed under my father's watchful eyes. Even then, I generally had more than enough material for the task at hand.

My grandmother had a particularly soft spot for the rabbits – they were big white furry creatures that lived in comfortably large, homemade wooden cages closed off with wire mesh doors. They were grass-fed. Most afternoons after lunch, my grandmother would go up and down the field, a large wire basket under her arm. The cats – we always had cats around the house – would accompany her, as cats do, at a distance making a show of their independent ways. She selected the best grasses and cut them with a red-handled serrated knife. The rabbits were particularly fond of dandelions and plantains. My grandmother had a theory that it was better for them to eat their grass dry; otherwise they risked catching life-threatening diarrhoea. So on rainy days, of which there were many in Normandy, the cut grass had to be left out to dry under the roofed-over open space beside the stables. That was also where the rabbit cages were kept and where the mother hens paraded their baby chicks. Baby chicks had to be fed special food that consisted largely of milk-soaked bread crusts. The trouble was that all the other chickens in the back garden would get quite worked up whenever they caught sight of my grandmother emerging from the kitchen holding the plate of baby chick food. So she had a system. She placed the plate under a circular cage propped up at one end with a brick, leaving just enough space for the chicks to crawl in. It was a good idea but my grandmother still had to stand guard so she could shoo away the big bossy roosters and pushy mother hens. Only then could the baby chicks go about their business of eating their milky mush in relative peace. She kept guard with a stick, on which she was increasingly dependent for walking around.

My grandmother had begun to suffer from rheumatism – the ugly, painful, kind that would eventually bend her hands and feet out of shape. In those days, pain did not mean very much to me. It was something that happened to grown-up people and I was a child. Children somehow belonged to a quite separate category of living beings.

She called each of her animals by name and yet there was nothing romantic about their existence. They were raised for the pot. She knew exactly how to catch a cockerel, bind its feet with twine, hold its head down, slit its jugular vein with the single stroke of a sharp knife, let it bleed away, pluck it while still warm, and finally empty it of its warm innards. Finding a rabbit's vein required even more skill and taking the life of a furry animal was somehow just that much harder. I watched all this in awe. My mother did not have it in her to do such things, still less my father. I admired my grandmother all the more for it.

4

Background To *The Fallen Idol*

I was, of course, still in Normandy with my beloved grandmother when the news came through that, following the quite extraordinary flight across the English Channel in the small prop plane, I would indeed be involved in making a film. I could tell that my parents were pleased. I was just about old enough to understand that there was money at stake and that, as far as they were concerned, this was a good thing. My parents had always talked quite openly about money – especially about how important it was to have some at hand – so that part was not particularly surprising.

I do not, however, remember being asked whether acting in a film was something I actually wanted to do, which is just as well because I would have found the question puzzling. The only thing I knew about films is that while we were living in London – during the war, mostly – my mother liked going to them and, in the absence of baby-sitters, she took me along with her. There were plenty of cinemas in Leicester Square playing black-and-white double features. I remember being quite bored. I would have been much happier left in the park playing with Pouffy.

Pouffy was now in Normandy and had joined the farm cats. He was not allowed to return to London because, according to my parents, the English had strong views about not wanting their dogs to catch the unspeakable diseases of French dogs. So Pouffy lived for the rest of his life in Normandy. My grandmother, whose opinion on the subject had not been asked, ended up caring for him and, of course, grew quite fond of him, but she did complain that Pouffy's long hair and dainty flat nose were ill suited to the rough and tumble of farm life. History had a way of repeating itself.

Pouffy, I learned later, had played a part in my being chosen to be a film star. He was a pretty dog and he and I were the best of friends. In London we had been pushed along for quite some time in the same pram. It was a good way of keeping us both out of trouble as my mother went shopping for groceries with her ration book or just taking us to Green Park for our daily exercise: much needed, of course, given the diminutive size of the flat.

We had been photographed together and separately a few times and, not surprisingly, we had both appeared in a book. I say 'not surprisingly' because by now my parents were well established in the book writing business. While some might write about things they dreamed up inside their heads this was not my parents' way of doing things: they wrote about what was under their noses, as it were. After the 1941 success of *A Farm in Normandy*, they had expanded the genre into writing about what life was like in Mayfair under the German blitz. The first book in this particular series was titled *A Village in Piccadilly* and came out in 1942. I have a copy of the first edition together with the original dust cover; an attractive montage of photographs – including one of me peering out of one of the flat's two windows – made to fit within the outline of a street map of central London. My yellowed copy includes a statement to the effect that it was produced in conformity with the British Government's war economy standards. My father is shown as the sole author. Although my father was meticulous about maintaining a complete library of books published under my mother's name – he was the kind of person who gave much thought to posterity – this particular book was missing at his death. Today I note with interest that the copy in my possession is a gift to me from a book-loving friend who lives in Maine and somehow acquired it by way of a secondhand bookseller in Johannesburg: but more later on why this particular book had been purged from my father's collection. The point is that Pouffy and I ended up having our photographs appear in a published book. We are both in our pram being pushed around Shepherd Market – the Mayfair neighbourhood my parents had christened as their 'village'. There is another picture of me to the left of the title page. I am looking out one of the flat's windows. Today I'm struck by its similarity with the opening scene of *The Fallen Idol*: a bemused and curious child looking in on the adult world.

Anyhow, the story goes that Sir Alexander Korda, the film impresario, was sitting around in his rather large Mayfair office - the one with the impressive wood panelling and the stunning view of Hyde Park - in the company of none other than the film director Carol Reed wondering how they might set about finding a child to act in their next film.

Who were these people and just why were they looking for an eight-year old child? It took me a very long time – almost 60 years – to reach the point in my life where I would feel comfortable asking such questions: not just comfortable asking them but also genuinely curious as to what the answers might be.

Korda was 54 at the time. He first came into his own as a film director in his native Hungary but, following the turmoil of the First World War, left Budapest and tried his luck in Vienna and Berlin and then, somewhat predictably, in Hollywood. Aggressively bright – he had a prodigious memory and was a gifted linguist – and ambitious, he grew disillusioned with Hollywood and after a stint in Paris finally settled in London. He staked his all in 1933 on a joyfully extravagant production starring Charles Laughton with the titillating title of *The Private Life of Henry VIII* which was an enormous success on both sides of the Atlantic. It established Korda as one of the leading lights of filmmaking second only to the likes of Charlie Chaplin and Sam Goldwyn and anointed him as the granddaddy of the now rejuvenated British film industry. The outbreak of war disrupted his career and caused him to return temporarily to Hollywood. He had the best of reasons for doing so since his Hungarian family had Jewish roots. The war over, he was back in London, owner of a film production studio and eager to start afresh.

Knighted in 1942 for having rescued British filmmaking from the doldrums of mediocrity, Korda approached Carol Reed. He believed in working with successful people and Reed's latest film *Odd Man Out* had just been released: the critics liked it. Although Reed had met with some early success in directing films in the mid 1930s, this was the film that established his reputation as a leading director. It is a disquieting, intelligent story fraught with moral ambivalence set in pre-war Ireland during the struggle for independence. The film's hero, Jimmy, is an awkward, star-crossed misfit played by none other than James Mason.

There is every reason to suppose that both Alexander Korda and Carol Reed had taken a strong liking to Graham Greene's storytelling. Greene was 43 at the time and already a well-established writer. He was known for his short stories and had published some of the novels – deeply psychological and reflective of his ongoing struggle with his adopted Catholic faith – that would account for his enduring reputation. Among these were *Brighton Rock* (1938), and *The Power and the Glory* (1940). Another of his books, *Stamboul Train* (1932), had been made into a Hollywood film. *Orient Express,* in 1934. This film – not to be confused with the 1974 Agatha

Christie blockbuster *Murder on the Orient Express* – turned out to be quite mediocre but was, nonetheless, the beginning of Greene's long career as a writer of stories that became remarkably successful films. Not only did he have a knack for telling stories that made good films but, remarkably, he took a strong personal interest in the highly technical business of producing convincing screenplays.

Reed had read quite a few of Greene's books and had taken a shine to *England Made Me*, a short novel published in 1935. The hero is a down-on-his-luck, morally shady character who ends up taking a job as bodyguard to an equally dubious Swedish financier. Greene's terse style makes for an engagingly dark narrative and the book is a very readable suspenseful page-turner. Korda, however, did not like it as much and, instead, suggested the briefest of short stories called *The Basement Room*, an even darker yarn loaded with psychological equivocation and theological innuendoes. It seems that when Reed read the story at Korda's suggestion he immediately sensed that this was a challenge worth taking up.

The Basement Room was first published in 1935. Graham Greene reputedly wrote it while on a slow boat bound for Liberia where he was to carry out some kind of spy mission on behalf of an anti slavery group. It was a journey that was to kindle within Greene a lasting fascination for provocative stories told in boldly extraneous settings and served as the backdrop to *Journey Without Maps*. Greene's cousin Barbara Greene accompanied him on this strange expedition. Also gifted and forthright in expressing her views, she published her own version of the adventure, *Too Late to Turn Back*, depicting her brooding cousin as a controlling and irascible companion.

The fact that Greene conceived *The Basement Room* on his first great journey into the unknown may have something to do with it being a stark, sombre tale whose hero, the ill-fated butler, fantasises about adventures set in a white-man dominated Africa in which he most likely never actually set foot. The story, and this is how it intersects in the oddest of possible coincidences with my own life story, is told through the eyes of a seven-year-old child.

When I first read it only a few years ago, having pulled it off the shelves of the local public library, it took me little more than an hour. The story, however, lingered with me like an intriguing but unwelcome dream that is both confusing and disquieting. Those were feelings that took me by surprise.

The story is about an only child, Philippe, who, for no very clear reason, is left behind for a couple of weeks by his parents in their London town house in the care of the butler and his wife. The house has a cavernous entrance hall with overhanging bannisters and a sweeping, larger-than-life staircase. Then there is the basement; hence the title of the story. At times the house feels very much as if it is an essential part of the story: almost like a ghostly personification of death foretold. The house also lends itself to the upstairs-downstairs theme that decades later became a staple of glossy British TV productions, except that the emphasis here is not so much on the stratification of British society in the period between the wars but rather with the child's experience of two separate worlds. The basement is the familiar, homely space within which he is able to give free rein to his admiration for the butler who, by force of circumstances, is his only friend: a friendship the butler fosters by filling the child's mind with extravagant stories set in a distant fictional and vaguely threatening Africa. The upstairs, in contrast, is the domain of cold, distant adults: not just of absent parents but, ominously, of the butler's wife who is its self-appointed guardian and personifies all that instills fear and hatred inside the head of a lonely, seven-year-old only child.

The fast-moving plot unfolds against the backdrop of an illicit affair between the butler – the child's hero – and a girl he passes off as his niece. The child, becoming aware of the girl's spurious identity, is charged with keeping her existence secret from the wife but ineptly fails to do so: the duplicitous ways of adults are beyond his ken. The girl's appearance, wrapped up within a sexuality of which the child is only vaguely aware, is a spoiler: she vies for the attention of his hero and disrupts the relationship he craves for. Meanwhile the wife, intent on catching out her philandering husband, makes a pretence of being called away to visit an ailing relative. The adulterous butler, the girl and the child are left to their own devices within the bleakness of the otherwise abandoned house. Ghostlike, the wife reappears at nightfall, rouses the child who has been sent to bed in his upstairs nursery, then confronts the adulterous lovers. In full view of the child, the exasperated butler pushes her over the bannisters, and her body crashes into the great emptiness below.

The child, in a bid to escape the horror and confusion of the adult world, makes a desperate dash into the maze of London's busy and darkened streets. The police eventually rescue him – a wandering, fearful, lost child – and accompany him back to his home. The child is terrified at the thought of coming face to face with the body lying lifeless in the entrance hall. But it is no longer there. The butler has sent his girl friend home and, acting the part of a distraught husband, tells the police how his wife accidentally tripped and slipped down the stone steps leading into the basement. He has moved the body into the basement for all to see. The butler's fate now depends on the child remaining silent, but it is too late. The child steps into the role of betrayer and the spell is irrevocably broken. There are no more heroes and the child has withdrawn from the world of emotions; it is a world given over to disillusionment and brokenness.

The chilling aspect of *The Basement Room* is that the child's withdrawal is permanent. Sixty years have gone by and the child, now on his deathbed, is a withered, emotionless human being who has failed to overcome the feelings of guilt induced by his betrayal of the only person he ever looked up to. There is no hope of redemption. *The Basement Room* is told as a flashback from the grown-up child's deathbed.

Sir Alexander Korda could tell this was a riveting story but he also knew the film business far better than most. The story goes that he asked Graham Greene and Carol Reed to get together and do what had to be done to turn *The Basement Room* into a screenplay that could be made into a box office hit: spookiness, adultery, lost innocence, and deceit are grist for the mill, but not unrelieved gloom. The two men apparently took rooms in a Brighton hotel for a couple of weeks and did their magic. There is irony to this. Greene knew Brighton quite well having used the seaside town as the setting for *Brighton Rock*: another *noir* tale with theological overtones that, although published before the war, had just been made into a film by one of Korda's rivals, Roy Boulting.

Greene and Reed quickly decided that it was not a good idea for the butler to heave his wife - scratching and hissing as though she were a demented cat - over the bannisters. Instead, they arranged for her, in her frenzied attempt to catch the lovers in an adulterous embrace, to slip accidentally from an upper floor window ledge and land lifeless at the bottom of the sweeping marble staircase around which the story plays itself out. Let it not be murder but rather let everyone, the child included, presume it to be murder. A clever ending could then be contrived to free the butler - a charming and pretentious rogue, perhaps, but not a murderer - from the clutches of an entire team of police sleuths. Before the clever ending, however, the detectives are misled into suspecting murder by the child's naïve and misguided attempt to cover up his hero's presumed crime.

The farmhouse in Normandy where I was born. This photograph was taken in 1938 but it still looks much the same.

My parents in Paris in the 1930s - one of the very few pictures I have of them together.

My father holding me in front of the Normandy farmhouse shortly after my birth in 1939. No other pictures exist of me as a baby or child with my father – the war came along and besides my parents didn't possess a camera!

Growing up on the Normandy farm. This was a press photo posed for
The Fallen Idol *publicity (I am dressed as I was in the film).*

*One of the four huge fireplaces in our Normandy farmhouse - the one with the
ornate pillars and little marble plaque indicating it was built in 1555.*

My mother, Madeleine, better known as the author Mrs Robert Henrey. This is a staged press photo of her; in reality it was my father's desk in their small Mayfair flat. My mother wrote most mornings sitting up in bed - with a shawl over her shoulders - using an old fountain pen and school exercise books.

Pouffy the Pekingese and me being wheeled around Shepherd Market. The picture also appeared in A Village in Piccadilly – *I don't know who is pushing the pram.*

This photo faced the title page of my father's book A Village in Piccadilly *published in 1942. I'm looking out into the courtyard from our Mayfair flat. Sir Alexander Korda's Production Executive noticed it in 1947: he referred to the possible lead as 'The Shepherd Market child'. It set the tone for the many shots in* The Fallen Idol *where I am looking from far off at an adult world that I still don't fully understand.*

On the set of The Fallen Idol *with director Carol Reed. Note the faux marble staircase - linoleum covered plywood - the kind of detail that intrigued my eight-year-old brain at the time.*

'Philippe' and his snake McGregor

Round the table, clockwise from me: Eric my stand-in, Peter Maxwell, Phil Brandon, Peggie McClafferty, Peter Broxup and Carol Reed. Guy Hamilton with his arm stretched out.

The main point of the original story - the child's loss of innocence brought about by adult ineptitude and duplicity - could then be preserved but without recourse to the kind of hyper gloom that causes him to spend the remaining 60 years of his life brooding over the damnation that surely awaits him. One observant critic also pointed out the 60 year look back built into the narrative structure of *The Basement Room* would, logically, have thrown the action of the film back to the end of the 19th century: something neither Reed nor Greene had any interest in doing. The child now has a reasonable chance of growing up normally - well almost!

Did I, in fact, grow up normally, people often ask me? Probably, but I cannot pretend that over the past 60 years I have not had my doubts.

It then made sense to rename the film. Reed and Greene came up with *The Lost Illusion* - not bad, but fortunately another renaming occurred before the film's release and it became known as *The Fallen Idol*. No doubt a more forceful title although apparently not to Graham Greene's liking.

Back in that Brighton hotel, Reed and Greene came up with a couple of other ideas. Greene wanted to incorporate a snake into the story. So into the script went a seemingly gratuitous piece about the child having a crush on a pet grass snake. The animal so irritates the butler's wife that she incinerates it behind his back, making a show of her intrinsic wickedness by harming the snake. Sixty years later, when I at last granted myself the luxury of thinking about such things, this struck me as a wonderful piece of irony. Who other than a tortured Catholic could have such fun by slyly introducing a whiff of original sin in a story about human folly?

The snake was called McGregor. Why such a dignified name for a grass snake? No knowing, except that it was the very same name Beatrix Potter had given years before to the gardener who had declared war on her lovable rabbits. Gifted writers delight in irony. Was I scared of the snake, I've been asked countless times over the years? Not really. I had spent time in the French countryside where there are plenty of dangers and knew instinctively that McGregor meant no harm.

The other change is attributed to Carol Reed. Had it not occurred to him, I would have spent the rest of the summer of 1947 undisturbed in Normandy and in the care of my grandmother. This great intrusion into my life would simply not have occurred. More to the point I would, most likely, have lived the rest of my life in blissful ignorance of the uncanny way in which pure chance can set in motion the unspooling of a thread that not only takes on a life of its own but also resists all attempts to sever it.

The marble staircase and the huge entrance hall are essential elements in the telling of the story: as much in *The Basement Room* as in *The Fallen Idol*. In 1935 there must have been more than a few English families rich enough to own a house in central London with such a staircase but this was 1947, and there was no reason to shoot the film other than in a contemporary setting. What bothered Reed was that in post-war Britain virtually no one could have afforded to live in so large a town house with servants, let alone with a sweeping majestic marble staircase. The Labour Party which had dealt Winston Churchill a painful political setback at the end of the war was now busy at work reshaping the social underpinnings of a near-bankrupt and exhausted nation. There was, for example, to be a National Health Service that would serve as a model for what was then left of the civilised world. In order to pay for all this, the marginal rate of income tax remained dizzyingly high: as high as it had during the worst years of the war.

Reed really wanted his sweeping marble staircase. He loved shooting scenes with the camera set at odd, provocatively slanted, angles and that is where staircases really come into their own. This was a trick with which he was so enamoured that he continued using it in *The Third Man*.

The solution was to transpose the setting to an embassy. There were plenty of embassies sporting lavish establishments in London's fashionable West End. Neither Reed nor Greene wanted to draw attention to any particular country so there was no need for flags or maps. Letting the child be the ambassador's son made the parents' temporary absence – another essential underpinning to the story – all the more plausible. Then there was the question of language – secondary perhaps but still an important detail. It would help if the child spoke with a touch of a foreign accent: not German, of course, this was 1947 but French, for example, would do just fine. There need not even be any inference that this was the French embassy. Was not French, after all, still a diplomatic language: decreasingly so, perhaps, but yes a slight French accent would do nicely. Actually, there was another good reason for settling on French.

The story revolves around the child and the butler but the girl also plays a major part. In the transposed setting, she is one of the ambassador's secretaries. Sir Alexander Korda wanted her to be elegant and sophisticated, as well as a beauty. This was a film with a more than adequate budget: all of £250,000. In 1947 a pint of beer in an upscale pub cost a shilling and £1,000 was a fair annual salary for a manager or even an experienced professional. Film budgets didn't include extravagant amounts for special effects and anyway this was a black-and-white film: £250,000 was money enough for a first class studio set, well-known actors and a team of top-notch camera technicians. The choice for the girl was Michèle Morgan. In 1938 – barely 18 at the time – she had played Jean Gabin's lover in *Quai des Brumes*, a film that is still thought of today as one of the great classics of French cinema. Having spent the war years in Hollywood she spoke excellent English, and in 1946 had been voted Best Actress at the Cannes Festival for playing the lead in the screen adaptation of André Gide's *La Symphonie Pastorale*. So there was already a French connection.

Clearly Korda wanted the best and a lot of thought must have gone into casting the lead part. The Old Vic Company had, since its rejuvenation by Sir John Gielgud in 1929, established itself as the pre-eminent upholder of the English acting tradition with, as might be expected, a particular emphasis on Shakespeare. The war, however, had taken its toll. The Old Vic theatre was severely damaged during the blitz and the company, in an attempt to keep going, was reduced to touring and finding temporary homes outside London. At the end of the war the company was invited back to London, granted exclusive use of the New Theatre in St. Martin's Lane on the understanding that it would one day move back to its original home and given over to a group of exceptionally talented actors among whom were Ralph Richardson and Laurence Olivier. The revival of the Old Vic turned out to be an enormous success and many critics went so far as to suggest that posterity would count both Richardson and Olivier among the best Shakespearean actors of all time. Then, at the beginning of 1947, both men had a falling out with the governors of the Old Vic Company and were peremptorily fired. Coincidentally Ralph Richardson was knighted in the same year in recognition of his excellence as an actor. It was the sacking from the Old Vic that provided Korda with the god-sent opportunity to sign up Ralph Richardson. In 1945 Richardson had put on a compelling performance as Falstaff in a stage production of *Henry IV*. It would be difficult to imagine a better credential for the role of the roué butler conceived of by Graham Greene.

So what about casting the child? There could not have been an easy solution to this particular problem. Given that the story is from beginning to end seen through the child's eyes there was a lot at stake. A poor choice ran the risk of jeopardising the entire production. This was not the kind of problem that could be solved by the traditional Korda approach of paying the price and going for established, well-proven talent. The problem rested with Reed more than with anyone else: it was he who would have to conceive of each step, each gesture, each intonation and then transpose them to a child capable of responding to such direction coherently and effectively. The logic in this approach was that while openness, a minimum level of intelligence and even a degree of competence were required of the child, it would be far better for him to have had absolutely no prior acting experience. It would be strictly up to Reed to supply the experience.

Back then to *A Village in Piccadilly*: the wartime literary effort written by my parents. It is not clear who, among all these important people, had actually read the book. According to my parents, it was William O'Brien, Korda's capable and resourceful production executive. O'Brien had apparently conducted a number of auditions but they were inconclusive. Out of frustration he came up with the idea of taking a chance on the little boy gazing out of the window who he called the 'Shepherd Market child'. There must, however, have come a point at which the book was shown around so that everyone had an opportunity to at least look at the pictures. It was obvious from the book's context that the child had been brought up speaking French as well as English. That is when the decision was made to get hold of my parents. Sir Alexander Korda was not the kind of impresario who would scrimp at the expense of chartering a private plane just to try out a hunch.

5

The Making Of *The Fallen Idol*

I am often asked just what it is that I remember from the actual making of the film. What memories do I have, for example, of Carol Reed and of the actors? What was it like having Carol Reed tell me exactly what to do day-in and day-out; was Michèle Morgan nice to me, what were people like Ralph Richardson and Jack Hawkins really like off-camera, did I remember meeting Graham Greene?

My answers to those questions must have been invariably disappointing because my most vivid memories are of the totally new surroundings in which I suddenly found myself rather than of those who peopled it. I was an eight-year-old and intensely curious in things, in what was their purpose and how they worked. Why do I remember so little about the people?

Some have suggested that growing up as an only child with no experience of schooling and very few friends of my own age, I must have been exceptionally lonely. If loneliness there was, and there must have been, I do not, at that time, remember experiencing it as something negative. There can, however, be little doubt that I was far more accustomed to interacting with adults than with my contemporaries. My parents had, until then, deliberately spared me the rough and tumble of the schoolyard. For my own good, they would have surely said.

My own parents were loving – to the point, I'm convinced, of being overly protective – but at the same time intent on moulding their only child into a persona of their own pleasing. That is, it has occurred to me many times, a risky course on which to embark. There may have been something reassuring and comforting about all this but it must have also sown within me an intense desire to assert my own personality: a feeling that permeated my relationship with my mother and – notwithstanding her living into her late 90s – stayed strongly within me till the very end. I am no psychologist but it probably played a role in my subsequent vigorous efforts to distance myself from *The Fallen Idol* experience.

At the time *The Fallen Idol* was made, I very much wanted to please the adults – my parents first among them – that peopled my little world and conform to their expectations. That seemed to be the way things worked. So being asked to step onto a film set where Carol Reed would be asking me to do his bidding down to the smallest detail may not have seemed to me at all unusual. There must have also been a certain emotional distancing involved in all this: perhaps it was my way of growing a protective shell, reinforced by my intense curiosity in things. I can think of countless times when, as a young adult, I made use of my then highly developed intellectual curiosity to distance myself from emotionally charged situations I was unprepared to face up to. For a reason I could never have anticipated, a day would come when that protective shell would have to be discarded: for the sake of my survival.

So I quite naturally took that curiosity with me to the totally new and largely make-believe environment of filmmaking. I have a very clear memory of the first scenes shot on location in the West End of London around Belgrave Square, the site of the imagined embassy around which Graham Greene and Carol Reed had adapted the script. I remember the huge, sputtering carbon arc lamps; the large square silver reflectors used to beam sunlight back onto the actors; the camera crew setting up the rails for the travelling trolley; the camera itself with a square hooded lens, surmounted by a film magazine and whirring wheels; the microphone boom; the continuity girl with her notepad and the makeup crew. I remember the scene in the neighbourhood teashop with Ralph Richardson and Michèle Morgan meeting secretly – a lovers' tryst I had unwittingly intruded on. I understood that there was something exciting and illicit about their meeting in this dingy little teahouse but that was only a vague, featureless, unemotional understanding. What I remember much more clearly was that in the script Ralph Richardson had tried to fob me off with a glass of milk and a raisin bun and that at the end of the scene he had given a couple of shillings to the woman behind the counter to pay for everything. There were other things that were real and imprinted themselves on my consciousness: the fact that the pasteurised milk did not smell of cow the way milk did in Normandy and that this was my first experience of raisin buns with their yellow mushy insides and glazed, sugar-sprinkled outsides.

With the exception of a few street scenes and an upbeat sequence at the London Zoo, where the lovers were hoping to have yet another secret tryst, the film was shot on studio sets. The London Zoo, however, left its mark on me. My parents were emphatically not the kind of people who frequented zoos so this was indeed a rare adventure. A zoo is of itself a make-believe world and here we were inside one filming a make-believe story. I could never have explained why but there was something thrilling about this realisation: a glimpse, perhaps, of the rush adults get when they experience some kind of epiphany.

Shepperton Studios had been built on what had once been the park surrounding a stately country house. It was within easy reach of central London and is today but a short distance from Heathrow. Studio life settled down to a Monday through Friday routine. My mother made the most of it. We had the use of an apartment within the studio complex and I had daily lessons from a governess who, according to my parents, knew nothing about teaching. My father joined us at weekends.

The idea behind a film set was, of course, immensely appealing to me. If the London Zoo had felt make-believe then this was the archetype of make-believe. The whole purpose, it occurred to me, was to improve on reality. I had from an early age taken particular delight in building imaginary castles out of the bits and pieces of cardboard my father brought home from work. I remember a particularly fine line drawing of a mediaeval castle included in a pre-First World War edition of Larousse's magnificent two-volume encyclopedia – a compendium of all that was civilised, seen through French eyes. The two large volumes were kept on the living room floor of the Mayfair flat. I spent so much time, sprawled on the rug, gazing at their plates – palaces, townhouses, steam-engines, horse-drawn carriages, military uniforms, maps of Imperial Russia and of colonised Africa – that my father finally gave up trying to protect them from my grubby, destructive little hands. The two volumes joined a half-dozen dog-eared teddy bears to become my most prized possessions.

And in Normandy the old farmhouse was heaven for an inveterate creator of imaginary worlds. The back garden and the barn were cluttered with pieces of wood of all shapes and sizes. My parents had hired a one-eyed out-of-work carpenter to build whatever furniture he could from these remnants. He was a tall, lanky, taciturn man who always wore a beret and enjoyed having me for company. He worked in the barn, mostly with traditional hand tools, spending hours sawing, sanding and joining old gateposts into tables, chairs and benches. Before long, the cottage was furnished with his rough-hewn, honest-to-goodness pieces. I loved watching him. He taught me about nails, hammers, pliers, how to saw along a more-or-less straight line and the secret of making a hole with an old-fashioned gimlet. I was far too impatient to be a good carpenter but he taught me to have reverence for wood. Some of those tumbled-down gateposts had been made of solid fine-grained oak: oak that could still be planed and polished into pieces that were a joy to smell and to feel. I also learned how thumbs and fingers get bruised and cut and why it was not always a good idea to run off and tell my parents about my latest mishap but rather to suffer in silence.

I had been given free rein over a small patch of the flower garden in front of the ancient farmhouse. It was under a cherry tree that had grown large enough to allow for a swing to hang from one of its branches: a piece of rough wood secured to two long chains. In good weather I would swing away – to excess – making myself as dizzy as I could, until I sensed the thrill of danger within the pit of my stomach as I careened down, caught in the exhilarating downswing of the freefall. It was there – beside the swing – that I built a miniature village. Its houses were made of all the odds and ends that came off the one-eyed carpenter's workbench. I would paint them to give them a half-timbered look and make thatched roofs out of straw.

The set at Shepperton Studios reproducing the ambassador's London mansion was just a grown-up version of my dreamy tinkering. It struck me as an object of great magnificence. It mimicked a palatial entrance hall; something I could only have known about from illustrated books. There, in the centre, was the huge marble staircase so essential to the story. It had to be vast – vast to the point of deluding the audience into believing that the adulterous butler played by Ralph Richardson had, in a fit of anger, and after having spent the night with the ravishing Michèle Morgan, pushed his dowdy wife Sonia Dresdel off the top step in the hope she would tumble down the stairs and he would be rid of her for good.

I was told this story repeatedly although I have reason to believe that I was bright enough to have grasped it the first time around. I did not really need to understand the bit about Ralph Richardson being adulterous or about his wife being dowdy, especially since Sonia Dresdel in real life was not in the least dowdy. It was enough for me to know that in the make-believe story she was mean – she had incinerated my pet snake – and that it was perfectly natural for Ralph Richardson to have preferred to spend the night with Michèle Morgan rather than with her.

There was absolutely no need for me to know that a lot of grown-ups thought that Graham Greene was an elegant and consummate storyteller and that it was thanks to him that the plot was so subtle. In other words, Ralph Richardson had not actually bumped Sonia Dresdel over the top step of the marble staircase. It was, however, important that I thought he had. Because I thought he had, I had therefore gone to great lengths to cover up something that had not happened and I had not done a very good job of lying. My lying led to confusing the police and almost condemning Ralph Richardson to a sticky ending for something he had not done. That was all rather complicated and I am not sure how important it was that I kept all those pieces sorted out in my head all the time.

No one seemed particularly interested in knowing what I really thought of all this but, if they had asked, I would have told them that I could think of a good number of far more exciting stories. I nonetheless fully realised that what counted here was that we were involved in make-believe. Make-believe just makes everything more real and exciting and there was, frankly, no need for Carol Reed to explain that one away. That was something I knew about.

It stands to reason therefore that what really interested me was the set. The magic here was that I could walk behind all this magnificence and see with my own eyes that it was an elaborate fake – a skin, as it were, stretched over a mere skeleton. The marble was speckled plasterboard, the black and white floor tiles over which Sonia Dresdel had collapsed were painted-over plywood and the brass mouldings and railings were common wooden dowels dipped in make-believe gold paint. The best part of all was that there were always carpenters and painters at the ready to change something at Carol Reed's behest. He was a demanding man who would go to great lengths just to enhance a camera angle or alter a layout so as to smooth the transition from one scene to the next. This is the part that I really looked forward to.

There were other sets at Shepperton Studios and ours was by no means the most elaborate. Visiting them was akin to travelling to foreign lands. My mother liked watching Vivien Leigh play the lead role in *Anna Karenina* and she was indeed very beautiful. We were interlopers on this particular set so we had to keep very quiet. I remember watching a gloomy snow scene and my mother explaining to me that the idea was to recreate something that was very Russian and therefore very moody, wintry and soulful. I was not at all sure what it was she was trying to tell me but I could certainly appreciate that it was far more special to be in the midst of a flurry of artificial snowflakes than to be outside experiencing the real thing. There was a life-size train on the set built entirely of plywood and painted black and, as might be expected since we were in Russia, the mood was definitely bleak. Then there was an even gloomier little man trudging around among the artificial snowflakes, tapping the train's wheels with a large hammer. The equally gloomy clanking sound would be added later – by then I had picked up enough about filmmaking to know about techniques like dubbing and lip-synching.

There was another elaborate affair going on in a nearby building that was set in Scotland and had to do with Bonnie Prince Charlie. I knew nothing about the Jacobite rebellion of 1746 and still less about David Niven in the lead role and the beautiful Margaret Leighton as Flora Macdonald – the woman who made it possible for the defeated prince to escape the clutches of the English. I did not need to.

What was hugely interesting to me was that the plot involved battles and soldiers in colourful 18th century period uniforms. It was not moody enough to suit my mother's taste but I found it altogether far more cheerful than the re-creation of Tolstoy's wintry wasteland, and I could have spent hours looking around at the props that included potted heather and real horses producing genuine droppings, just like those threatening carthorses in Normandy. I remember in particular that the set makers had tried their hand at perspective. So, for example, to convey the vastness of a battlefield, they had lined up successive rows of cannons, each row being made up of ever-smaller cannons with the barrels of the most distant being no more than a few inches long. As always, everything was made of plywood.

I grew to love this make-believe world and it was this that made the deepest impression on me. The actors were, by and large, distant figures that I came to know later more through repeatedly watching the film rather than from experiencing them off camera. There were, however, a couple of exceptions. Sonia Dresdel is, of course, the villain in the story and, according to the script, is appropriately scheming and vindictive. She sets out to frighten and manipulate me into betraying the lovers. She is a Queen of the Night lording it over a cold, impersonal world far removed from the cosiness of the basement within which I am free to indulge fantasies inspired by Ralph Richardson's bogus reminiscences of darkest Africa. But off camera, I remember Sonia Dresdel as a caring and kind person who had time to pay attention to me, an eight-year-old child, lonely and somewhat adrift within a busy world peopled by distant adults.

I would later find out that Sonia Dresdel was, at the time, an already accomplished actor. She was 38, and had made a name for herself both on the London stage in a production of Ibsen's *Hedda Gabler*, and also in a highly successful film *While I Live* (1947): a haunting film where Dresdel plays the domineering older sister of a gifted pianist who falls to her death while sleepwalking along a cliff top in a deserted part of Cornwall.

I had much the same impression of Dora Bryan – at the time a little known supporting actor – who in *The Fallen Idol* played the whimsical role of a young prostitute in the film's sole police station scene. I also remember Denis O'Dea, the chief detective investigating the death of the butler's wife in the second half of the film. He was a kindly Irishman who seemed to have time for the small child that I was. He had already worked with Carol Reed as the tough-minded detective in *Odd Man Out*.

The making of the film stretched far beyond its original timeframe. The fault, apparently, lay with Carol Reed who turned out to be a perfectionist and had, most likely, greatly underestimated the time it would take to direct a child. I do, in fact, remember certain scenes having to be shot over and over again but, as far as I was concerned, there was nothing notably constraining or even remotely unpleasant about the repetitiveness of it all. An example often given of Carol Reed's fastidiousness and resourcefulness is the film's opening scene where the child is looking down from an upper staircase into the vast entrance hall below watching his hero Ralph Richardson orchestrating the dusting and ordering of the ambassadorial household. I was asked to smile, to show that I was enjoying myself and taking pleasure in watching Ralph Richardson do his magic with the servants, and that my little mind was indulging itself in secret fantasies. I would, for reasons unknown to me, have none of this smiling business. In desperation Carol Reed had a magician brought in with a suitcase full of tricks. I was the poor man's sole audience and his sole objective was to make me smile as the camera rolled. The incident became part of the Carol Reed legend: no ingenuity off limits and no expense spared to get the child to do the maestro's bidding.

Working on a film set was heaven compared to being subjected to my parents' lessons. My impression is that Carol Reed made use of whatever mannerisms were already mine. In that sense I was never asked to act out of character. I have every reason to believe that I was not particularly good at remembering my part. Past a few lines of dialogue, I would simply forget the words I had been asked to memorise. That was not just due to my relatively young age. In time I became enough of an actor to master the diction, inflection, the mannerisms of others, and even the expression of feeling, but I never did acquire the ability to learn long texts by heart. I doubt I would have made it through a proper audition.

There was a routine to studio work. Everybody there was doing a job and the pay was good. I even vaguely remember feeling that way myself, no doubt reflecting remarks I had overheard my parents make. The cafeteria served three meals a day – I grew fat and had to be put on a diet – my mother took me for walks, my father appeared at weekends and we, together with the studio staff, were entitled to a free film each week. One of the scenes from *The Private Life of Henry VIII* made a particularly strong impression on me: there was Charles Laughton dressed up as King Harry, banqueting with his boisterous cronies, and throwing chicken bones to the dogs. That was living! My mother loved all the attention and I know the extra money pleased her and my father no end. I missed my grandmother, but I knew that the ancient farmhouse would still be there when this was all over.

I was right – but things did not just go back to the way they had been before. There was a sequel to this film story and it was a long one.

6

Coping With Success

The first night of *The Fallen Idol* was in London in September 1948 – I had turned nine by then – and it met with more success than could have been reasonably anticipated. The critics loved it, found the story to be a clever one written by a master of the short story genre and it had, by the standards of the late 1940s, benefitted from a generously large budget, the producer was a perfectionist, and the actors well known. It was, however, natural for the film critics and the press to focus on the child through whose eyes the story was told. I was featured in numerous articles in the daily press and in magazines. Photographs inevitably accompanied the articles: of the child, of course. Instant celebrity has journalistic appeal. It had come about overnight. People stopped me in the streets, pointed at me, asked for autographs, and put questions to me.

I do not have in my possession any of the numerous newspaper clippings from the period: the ones my parents had kept in large folders were thrown out long ago. A friend, however, many years ago gave me a copy of the December 13th 1948 issue of *Life* magazine. I have kept it in the bottom of a drawer but do occasionally look at it. The editor-in-chief is Henry Luce, the newsstand price is 20 cents and it features General Dwight D. Eisenhower's book *Crusade in Europe*: 'Ike', smiling and in uniform, is on the front cover. Inside there is a story about the Harry Truman White House – Ike did not become president until 1953. I love old magazines and this one is a bumper issue, given that there are barely ten shopping days left before Christmas. There is a full-page Santa Claus ad inviting readers to give away Chesterfield cigarettes by the carton: 'Sock 'em with a load of good cheer' says the caption.

The reason my friend gave me the magazine is that on page 103 there begins a four-page review of *The Fallen Idol* under the heading 'A Staggering

Performance'. There are six photographs, three of them showing Carol Reed directing me, and the child is in all six. It is a long, thoughtful article, marvelling at Carol Reed's skill and patience and making much of his foresight in choosing a child with no prior acting experience. The articles quote from a reviewer writing for the *Daily Mail*: 'I am on my knees before little Bobby Henrey who carried the whole structure upon 8-year-old shoulders and is never for one instant a child-actor but always a child...' Heady stuff indeed that, even today, I do not find it easy to read without sensing a degree of embarrassment. What also struck me about the article is that the film had not yet reached the United States: it was scheduled for distribution on the East Coast in early 1949.

There was more. At that time the British film industry sponsored an annual extravaganza that went by the name of The Royal Command Performance. Held in one of the large cinemas in London's West End, it was always patronised by royalty. The success of *The Fallen Idol* had been such that I was given the honour of presenting the Queen with a bouquet at the 1948 event at the Empire, Leicester Square. Her husband – King George VI – would normally have accompanied her but that evening he was sick. To my great surprise a British Pathé video of the event is posted on YouTube: among the guests are Elizabeth Taylor, Vivian Leigh, Myrna Loy and, irony of ironies, Ronald Reagan. I come in almost at the end of the YouTube clip with my bouquet, bow just a little bit awkwardly – the Queen takes the bouquet from me and then graciously shakes my hand – then my mother who is standing behind me comes up and gets her chance to curtsy. I press the pause button and here is this awesome image on my computer screen: my mother would have loved it were she still alive. In 1948, my mother was 42, she wore an elegant formal silk evening gown and she looked very attractive. My father was watching from the sidelines wearing what he had always worn: a Saville Row-cut, double breasted suit, a white silk shirt and an Old Etonian tie. That was his uniform. He increasingly liked operating from the sidelines and directing my mother as she moved within the limelight. I did not at the time understand why any of this was happening.

How did I react to all this hoopla? Did it, I am asked to this day, change my life? Did I become a spoilt brat? These are challenging questions. It is impossible not to be affected by adulation. People treat the successful in subtly deferential ways. I was a cute child and people – all adults, of course – went out of their way to be nice to me and make complimentary remarks. Some of this could not help rubbing off on me: we humans cannot avoid warming to the lavishing of praise. I would soon enough find out that being in the eye of the crowd is very much a double-edged sword. Exposure to the expectant gaze of others inevitably nurtures feelings of vulnerability. It is in the nature of things that those gazed upon sooner or later imagine themselves to be targets. They actually often are. For now, though, there were no such clouds on the horizon.

In other ways nothing much had changed. My parents were not about to move from their dingy little flat with the fancy Mayfair address. Upper tax brackets were punitively high and even though the extra money must have helped, I do not remember it making much of a difference to the way we lived. I had still never attended school and the only meaningful contact I had had with children of my own age was while living in France - and even that was minimal. I had merely been allowed to play with those in the neighbourhood. I therefore had next to nothing to go by and, consequently, little understanding of the extent to which this was a strange and unusual experience. If anything the success of the film isolated me even more from those of my own age. I was an object of curiosity within an adult world.

My parents were increasingly taken up with their literary ambitions. During the filming they had worked on a book about the making of the film and had called it *A Film Star in Belgrave Square*. I grew up intensely disliking the title and made a point of not reading it. It was only when the time came for me to write the final chapter of this book that I took care of this piece of unfinished business - almost exactly 65 years after its publication in early 1948.

I was allowed to go back to France so I could be with my grandmother but life had become more complicated. Reporters came to the farmhouse and my mother and I spent a few weeks at the famous Ritz Hotel in Paris, so the film could be dubbed in French using my own voice. I was still not sent to school.

It was at about this time that the formula my parents had hit upon for their joint literary production underwent a significant transformation. My mother came up with the idea of writing about her childhood years in Paris. I have a memory of her writing as she sat up in bed in the ancient Normandy farmhouse, propped up with pillows and a shawl over her shoulders. It was the upstairs room in which I was born and has the east facing view over the valley. She wrote her story with a Parker fountain pen filling, seemingly effortlessly, one exercise book after the other. She wrote in the very same fine-lined exercise books she used as a child and in which, before her, generations of French schoolchildren had done their homework. She had a round, even hand and rarely ever scratched out a word. It turned out to be an engaging story.

I figured out later that the success of *The Fallen Idol* had played a significant role in bringing about this change in my parents' literary strategy. It had made it financially possible for my father to give up his job in London – I have no way of knowing which newspaper he had been working for at the time – and for both my parents to spend the best part of a year in Normandy. It was, for my parents, a kind of sabbatical.

My mother had a prodigious memory and a fine eye for detail. She wrote unabashedly about real people. What she wrote had all the appeal of a rags-to-riches story – a precociously intelligent but uneducated young girl emerging from the slums of Paris, meeting a prince charming, and being introduced to a new life in a new country. She, of course, wrote in French, but this time the story was exclusively about her so even though my father, as always, thoroughly edited the text and rendered it into polished English, it made sense to publish the book under her own name. While she wrote in bed in the morning at one end of the house he tapped away at his Smith Corona for much of the day in his own room at the other end. My grandmother was downstairs cooking meals and taking care of the house. I, of course, was with my grandmother: my ally and protector against both my parents' sporadic efforts to school me. I could not help being aware of occasionally flaring tempers and hurt feelings.

The book was titled *The Little Madeleine* and published in early 1951 under my mother's married name, Mrs Robert Henrey, with the emphasis on the 'Mrs'. This was a way of tying the new book to all those previously published under my father's name.

The Little Madeleine proved to be by far the most successful book to come out of my parents' literary partnership. It went through a series of reprints and, while it did not make my parents rich, it established my mother as a reputable author with a significant source of predictable royalty income. From that moment on not only did my father never publish another book under his own name, but he deliberately engaged in a campaign designed to give the impression that my mother was in fact the author of all the books he had previously published. Thanks to the success of *The Little Madeleine,* the publisher readily agreed to reprint a number of my parents' earlier books. Rather than just reprinting them, my father combined some of the earlier titles and attributed the authorship to Mrs Robert Henrey. It was thus that their earliest joint book, *A Farm in Normandy* (1941), and *The Return to the Farm* (1947) were revised and recast into a new title *Madeleine Young Wife* (1954 in New York and 1960 in London). My father did much the same with the books he had published describing life in London during the war years, including *A Village in Piccadilly* (1942) with the photographs that unexpectedly led to my becoming a child actor. These wartime titles were eventually reworked, combined and published, under my mother's name, as *London Under Fire* in 1969.

I was not indifferent to all this manipulation. As a child trying to figure out how the world worked, none of this seemed very fair or even rational. I was irked by my father's habit of placing my mother on a pedestal and I did not want to hear from him that she was one of the great woman writers in the tradition of George Eliot or Mrs Gaskell. I tried to deal with this whole messy make-believe by distancing myself from it, as indeed I had from some of the increasingly unwelcome aspects of having been a child actor. I did not like the idea that, to me, my father was somehow demeaning himself. As far as my mother was concerned she just seemed to attribute it all to my father's innate eccentricity and to his peculiar but strongly held belief that women are naturally disposed to literature and that certain aspects of their writing are qualitatively superior to that of men. Being the practical person she was, she ultimately gave him credit for doing whatever he could to sell as many books as possible. My parents never had enough money so that every little bit helped. Besides, she probably found all this flattering.

It is only recently that I have felt emotionally robust enough to read some of my parents' literary output and piece together what kind of emotional impact it has had on my own life. I still do not like the fact that my father tried to recast past events. Out of curiosity, I decided to compare the original text of *A Farm in Normandy* with the reworked version of the same book included in *Madeleine Young Wife*. My first surprise was that I could not find a copy of *A Farm in Normandy* among my father's books: not among those in his study in the ancient farmhouse, nor among the books he sent to me for safekeeping in Connecticut. I had to resort to a second hand bookseller located on the Internet to obtain a copy. My father had purged it from his library.

My second surprise – although I should have known better – is that the narrator in the second version is now my mother and not my father. To me that strikes a decidedly off-key note. In the original, my father speaks of having fallen in love with the Normandy farm and buying it even though he is fully aware of the storm clouds beginning to gather over Europe. In the second version, it is my mother who expresses – word-for-word – those very same sentiments. The one thing that was perfectly clear within our family is that it was my father who had fallen in love with the ancient farmhouse of my birth and emphatically not my mother – who regarded it as something of a land of exile away from her beloved London. It was only after my father's death in 1982 that she began to cling to it as a refuge against an uncertain world – only then did she make it really hers.

So, yes, I still have those old misgivings although, as I advance in age, I feel more acutely than ever the need to be reconciled to the things my parents did. Life is, after all, a confusing struggle. I can also imagine that promoters and publicity departments most likely had a hand in this and that my parents just went along with what seemed to make sense at the time. I increasingly give them grudging credit for muddling through it all.

7

Why Not Another Film?

I am often asked why I never went on to become a professional actor. Why only one film? Why did I turn my back on success?

The success of *The Fallen Idol* was such that my parents were approached by a lot of people with all kinds of proposals: some were outlandish and others went nowhere. I sense that my parents were also quite confused by the way things had turned out. They were, to an extent, faced with a stark choice: have their only child go back to a normal life or embark wholeheartedly on an acting career. The idea of having me 'go back' to a normal life was a bit unrealistic. My upbringing had been so unconventional that, arguably, I had never experienced anything really normal. My father did want me eventually to go to school but very much on his own terms. His own upbringing had been unconventional enough. Having spent his childhood in the London suburban vicarage tutored, thanks to his mother's wealth, by his French governess, he was sent, at 13, to Eton. He was immensely proud of having been to Eton and claimed that it was during the four years he spent there that he taught himself to write. So much so that by 18 he firmly believed he had no further need for formal education. If that was his model for me – and I believe it was – then there was really no place for a wholehearted and immediate embrace of acting.

Having said that, my parents still could not quite make up their minds. Money was, after all, a big plus. Even if the right thing really was for me to be sent to school, might it not be possible to play for time: wait a little longer? Just long enough to see if something interesting cropped up. In the meantime, my parents had decided they could usefully use the time exploring the idea of a book based on my mother's childhood memories: hence the sabbatical year spent in Normandy. But I have no recollection of being asked how I felt about any of this.

Something did show up. Sir Alexander Korda's arch rival, the Rank Organisation, was then the largest British film production company. The story goes that there were people at Rank interested in making a film based on a script by Aldous Huxley involving a musical prodigy: a phenomenally precocious child – a Mozart clone, no less – is entrusted to a couple so he can be tutored to become one of the world's great conductors. Predictably, the tutors turn out to be demoniacal fanatics and the child is sequestered and cut off from his prior life. There was, so I gathered, a happy ending! My parents were approached and were tempted enough to listen to the terms of the offer: the more so perhaps because Korda had, so they felt, been desultory in signing me up for another film. The upshot of this was that when Korda heard that Rank had approached my parents, he immediately stepped in and made his own offer, not for a specific film but with a contract designed to prevent his competitors from signing up the star of *The Fallen Idol*. I know my parents liked the money part and so they signed and waited. They did not, of course, really mind the waiting since they were getting on with their own literary careers working on *The Little Madeleine*.

Alexander Korda was naturally free to do as he pleased: the contract bound him to no particular script, to no particular producer and to no specific actors. I suspect he might have been tempted to do nothing. Why, after all, risk another film with a child actor? It is difficult to imagine how the success of *The Fallen Idol* could have been duplicated without a producer of Carol Reed's stature. Besides, *The Third Man* – yet another Korda-Reed venture – had just come out and the critics had gone wild. That would be yet another impossibly hard act to follow.

There would, as it turned out, be a sequel. In retrospect it all seems a bit improbable but here is how it came about. Despite the devastation wrought by the rise of Nazism, Korda still had strong connections in Central Europe. After leaving his native Hungary in the 1920s, he had worked in a number of European capitals, including Vienna. He had a soft spot for Austria. At the end of the war Austria, together with Germany, had been carved up into four separate zones controlled respectively by the United States, Russia, Britain and France. While by 1949 it was clear that the German Soviet zone would transform itself into East Germany and remain behind the Iron Curtain, the situation in Austria was far less favourable to Russia and the situation remained tense and unresolved. The upshot was that all of the four powers temporarily occupying Austria remained in place: Vienna itself being carved up among the four. Korda had friends in Austria and most likely financial claims on currency that could only be spent within the country. Why not make a film there?

In the light of subsequent events it almost seems as if, by picking Karl Hartl as the film's director, Korda had simply wanted to do an old friend a good turn. Hartl was well enough known in Austria, had made some fine films during his long career and even owned a small studio in Vienna that would come in handy for the making of a film. Outside of Austria, however, it is doubtful many people had heard of him.

Under Hartl's direction, Korda had assembled a motley crew. Gene Markey, an American already in his mid 50s was to be the scriptwriter. In fairness, Gene's far greater claim to fame was his fine war record as a naval officer. Among the actors was Robert Shackleton, a relatively unknown American, and Sebastian Cabot, a physically huge man who was to achieve a degree of fame in Britain as a comedian and character actor. Finally there were a number of Austrians who, given the dire economic conditions of the time, must have been grateful to have paying jobs. One among them, Oskar Werner, would eventually emerge from obscurity. François Truffaut chose him years later to take the role of Jim in *Jules et Jim*: in my opinion one of the great films of all time.

Gene Markey concocted a flimsy story about a child pianist - a prodigy - who is kidnapped by a bunch of inept crooks, hidden in the Austrian Tyrol, then taken to Vienna and finally reunited with his family. It was more a comedy than a tragedy and, to add insult to injury, there was nothing remotely noteworthy about the saccharin title of *The Wonder Kid*.

The film was shot for the most part in Austria. The warm late summer months of 1949 were spent shooting on location in the Tyrol near Innsbruck and then the film crew moved to Vienna and continued to work up to and beyond Christmas. I lived in hotels with my mother and had yet another governess. My mother had finished the manuscript of *The Little Madeleine* and my father was back in London no doubt putting the finishing touches to the book.

What I remember best was the stunning beauty of the Tyrolean Mountains, but something else of a quite different nature also struck me. By now I was 10, old enough to be aware of the Cold War and it was in Austria that I first saw American and Soviet soldiers. One incident, in particular, struck me. Shortly before Christmas we had mistakenly been taken to a sound recording studio - the Vienna Philharmonic was recording a Mozart piano concerto for inclusion in the film's soundtrack - located in a section of the

Soviet zone from which foreigners were excluded. I could read the anxiety on the faces of those who were with me. We were probably not in any real danger but it was my first brush with the fear bred by the mere existence of a police state.

The beauty of the Tyrol, the charm of Vienna and a soundtrack graced with Mozart and Beethoven piano concerti played by the Vienna Philharmonic were not enough to salvage the film. There is a measure of confusion surrounding its release: some suggesting that outside Austria it was never put into full commercial distribution. Maybe all Korda ever wanted to do was to prevent my parents from signing me up with a competitor and do a good turn to a group of people he was in a position to help out with a pay cheque.

And what of the film I could have been in had my parents signed the contract with the Rank Organisation rather than with Korda? Rank did make the film, it was called *Prelude to Fame* and it came out in 1950. The strange thing about it is that Aldous Huxley's story line is bizarrely similar to that of *The Wonder Kid*. It is set in Italy rather than in Austria but the child is also a musician – a conductor. While there are some differences – such as his being sequestered by his tutors rather than kidnapped by crooks – there is, however, the same happy ending. The Rank Organisation signed up Jeremy Spenser to play the role of the prodigy. I have no idea whether the film was successful. I doubt it, though. Spenser is two years my senior and he became a professional actor with numerous parts to his credit.

When the filming was over, I was old enough to know that something had gone wrong and this was no *Fallen Idol*. It was, I suppose, my first brush with failure. My parents must have shrugged it off. They had done quite well financially out the arrangement and they had managed to bring out yet another book. This one was titled *Journey to Vienna* and significantly, was published under my mother's name. It is basically a travel book with titbits about the making of the film and some interesting glimpses of daily life in post war occupied Austria. It is not great literature but it is good enough.

It was, in any event, the end of my film career.

8

School After Filming

I was, at the close of the *Journey to Vienna* episode, fast approaching my 11th birthday. My brief film career had clearly come to an end and the time had come for my parents to face reality: most particularly in terms of what should and could be done regarding my education. It was decided that I should follow in my father's footsteps and be sent to Eton. Not, as my parents were about to find out, a very realistic goal for a child who not only had never attended school of any kind, but also had experienced a highly unconventional childhood. My parents were told they would have to send me to a preparatory boarding school as a precondition to my taking an entrance examination.

I was not given any choice in the matter and look back on this first experience of schooling as one of the most unpleasant periods of my life. This was Northaw, near Ashford in Kent, a small school – strictly for boys – run on almost military lines by a headmaster who had been an officer in the British army and insisted on being referred to as Major. Northaw was some 60 miles south of London and in those days parents were expected to deliver their children to a train, kiss them goodbye and not see them again for several months. The school was in what had been a private country house, the rambling buildings were cold in winter, the food was dismal and I felt my parents had completely abandoned me. The school placed great emphasis on sports and on character building. The primary aim of discipline, including the occasional cane whacking, was to instill character and toughness. The world of sports was totally alien to me. My father had no interest whatever in rugby or cricket, still less in soccer that in those days was regarded as suitable only for the lower classes. I had never played a team game of any sort, had no prior experience of the rough and tumble of institutional sports, had poor hand-eye coordination and was discovered after a few months to be developing extreme near-sightedness.

Parents who could afford private boarding school education were expected to send their children to such institutions around the age of seven. I, on the other hand, was already 11 and woefully unprepared for the experience. It was painful on many different levels. I had not developed the survival skills children acquire through living in close proximity to each other and as an only child my social interactions until then had taken place almost exclusively with adults. And the fact that I had acted in a highly publicised film made me different. Children have a natural tendency to reject, attack and exclude those who are different, especially when the difference is attributable to something that is foreign to the schoolyard culture. I was therefore something of an ugly duckling, fair game for teasing and ridicule. No one had prepared me for this, so instead of making light of the unwanted attention and letting it run its natural course, I all too often overreacted and angrily counter-attacked against impossible odds. My problems were compounded by the fact that I was a small child and not especially physically resilient.

I began to regret the fact that fate had made me into a child actor. Why could I not just be ordinary, like everyone else, adept at kicking a ball around, a wily survivor in a treacherous world and otherwise quite unremarkable? From that moment on, I did everything possible to put my acting career behind me. I resolved to never, ever mention the fact that I had been the star actor in *The Fallen Idol* and did whatever I could to avoid the subject. This was not just a passing phase, a temporary tactic designed to get me through a tough situation that would eventually resolve itself. On the contrary, I now realise that I had adopted a long-term self-preservation strategy and kept it in place during most of my adult life. It had become a taboo, painful subject I consistently chose to avoid. But these were complex feelings, and paradoxical because, whenever the subject came up, as inevitably in time it did, I unfailingly experienced a touch of pride. Fame, it seems, is a potent drug.

At school, I kept my spirits up knowing that there were holidays. At the end of each of the academic year's three terms my parents sent me back to Normandy. They did so immediately since there was no room for me in the London flat. My grandmother was always there to welcome me and make me feel as if I was the most important person in the world. Each of my visits to Normandy was a reprieve, and a return to my roots; a return to a constant, nurturing, presence.

There were three bedrooms in the ancient farmhouse. The middle one was mine. It was the smallest of the three but by far the most beautiful. It had a fireplace; one of the four that was part of the 16th century limestone structure, around which the half-timbered section of the house had been erected. It was a shallow but very wide fireplace flanked with columns and capitals on each side: rough-hewn but seen through a child's eyes as quite magical. My father had, before the war, caused its flue to be blocked off, and had more recently had a bookcase built into it. I used its shelves for books – my books, not anyone else's – but it was, above all, home to my Teddy bears. Each had a name and they sat nestled among the books. I had outgrown soft toys, of course, but this was also their home and they had as much right to live there as I did. It was the prettiest room because each of its four walls was half-timbered and no attempt had been made to layer them over with plaster. That meant that when the wind blew it made its way through the cracks. That was not all that important since the room was above the kitchen. The floorboards were broad and ancient and so ill fitting that the warm air rose from the Aga below and, in spite of the draughts, kept the room reasonably cosy. It was furnished with a narrow bed and an old-fashioned cupboard – old Norman houses never had built-in closets so that freestanding cupboards built of stained oak were a necessity. That was about it: there really was no room for anything else.

There was, however, a small round table beside the bed on which I kept a radio. The radio was special. I had been given it years ago by the local electrician. He was a kindly man who also happened to be an accomplished fossil collector. He kept his fossils in the back of his shop and I loved gazing at the ammonites, the spines of belemnites, and numerous fragments of a dinosaur jaw he had lined up on shelves among the bulbs and electrical fittings. The Germans, in their hasty retreat in June of 1944, had left behind all kinds of gear, including the radio. It bore the stamp of the Luftwaffe, the German Air Force, had earphones and the old fashioned lamps inside its grey steel casing hummed gently. I was old enough that now all these things already reminded me of my earlier childhood – a less complicated time about which I was prematurely nostalgic.

My grandmother told me stories, cooked exciting dishes and kept my spirits up. She was increasingly arthritic so that she was no longer able to walk long distances. Even though the shops in what we called the village were only about a mile away, the hill down to them was steep. It was now my responsibility to shop and bring back the groceries. I went everywhere by bike. I had never felt freer than on a bike.

I dreaded having to go back to London. There was a routine to the miserable business of having to go back to school that included the night spent on a mattress in the Mayfair flat and being taken to Waterloo station for the afternoon train.

To make matters worse, I was academically unprepared for school life. My parents' effort at home school and the lessons given me by a succession of governesses paid for by the film companies had yielded mixed results. I spoke French fluently and wrote both French and English well, but found other subjects such as mathematics and Latin quite irksome. I was simply not a disciplined student. When, around the age of 13, the time came for me to take an elaborate written exam for Eton, I failed it and my parents were told I would not be given a second chance.

My father was deeply hurt. He must have realised my filmmaking career, brief though it had been, had played a part in this failure, but even so he felt betrayed. Eton had nurtured his identity and he felt connected to its rich history – never in his life had he worn a tie other than an Old Etonian tie – and now it had let him down.

For me this was also the most unpleasant of times: my second brush with failure. It was hard not to attribute at least part of this misery to the events that had led to *The Fallen Idol;* or did it have more to do with that experience of *Paradise Lost* that haunts the human psyche?

Panic ensued. The British class system would have made it very difficult for my father to come around to the idea of sending me to a State school. I could, I suppose, have continued my schooling in France, but would have had great difficulty switching from one system to another.

During the war years spent in London, my mother had made a number of friends, among them a French woman some ten years her senior. She was divorced from her English husband and had lost her only child, a son. My mother remembered the details of the tragedy. The son was attending Downside, a well-known Catholic public school in Somerset run by the Benedictine Order. He was about 16 at the time. He and a friend decided they would take off on a motorbike belonging to one of the teachers. Within a short time of starting up the bike, they crashed into a truck and the son of my mother's friend was killed instantly. The young man was buried in the monks' cemetery beside the abbey church. My mother's friend, hearing of my parents' predicament, offered to write to the school's headmaster recommending he consider me for admission. She felt she was, in a very real sense, owed a favour.

When, much later in my own life, I had reason to reflect on what this woman had done, it occurred to me that she had, even if subconsciously, found a way of dealing with part of her own enduring grief, by giving to someone else what she had wanted to give to her own son.

Yes, I would be considered for admission but not before being sent back to the militarily inclined preparatory school so I could take another of those daunting exams. Then something very odd happened. The place went up in flames. Literally! I remember being in my pyjamas on a warm summer night sitting on the lawn and watching the great manor house crumble under a smothering of flames with fire engines standing by hopelessly. That was the end of the school except for those of us who were to sit exams. We, the lucky few, were billeted out among the local inhabitants and taught in what had been the stables attached to the manor house. It was a thoroughly enjoyable experience: gone was the irksomeness that had made a misery of the place. I did well enough in the exam.

My parents were immensely relieved to have found a reputable school willing to accept me, but there was nonetheless the tricky question of religion.

My father had been brought up in a Church of England vicarage. I never knew my grandfather, the Rev. Selby Henrey, since he died of a stroke shortly after the outbreak of war, but I have photographs of him. He looks stern, unsmiling and wears a dark suit and a clerical collar. He is a bit chubby but otherwise rather like my father with his solid Anglo-Saxon good looks, squared-off face, eyes that I imagine to be blue and blonde hair that is beginning to recede. I have clearly inherited some of those same genes: they have asserted themselves with the passage of years. He had, according to my father, simple tastes and his sole claim to intellectual fame was the publication of a collection of witty anecdotes attributable to Oxford and Cambridge worthies. There was irony in this since he himself had never had the opportunity to attend a university. My father credited his mother Euphemia with having all the brains in the family. It was she, he claimed, who wrote my grandfather's sermons and, even though my father thought of them as boring and overly lengthy, he was proud of her.

I remember our Sunday visits during the war years to my grandmother, now a widow, in Guildford but I remember her much better from her photographs. My father admired his mother and felt an affinity with her that was absent from his relationship with his father. In one of her photographs, she is sitting with a woollen shawl around her shoulder. She is already an old lady, kind-looking, dignified and slightly hunched. She is fine-featured and her face is angular. That is how I remember her. I do not remember her ever speaking to me, although she clearly did.

My grandmother had taught herself Greek and Hebrew and was widely read. She was a woman of deep faith. Her own grandmother was Hannah, one of the daughters of Nathan Mayer Rothschild, the founder of the English branch of the famous banking family. Hannah had married an English aristocrat, Henry Fitzroy, who rose to political prominence as speaker of the House of Commons. It was a happy marriage and although Hannah became a Christian she remained on close, affectionate terms, with the Rothschild clan. The couple had two children, a son who, having fallen off a horse while still a child, was paralysed and eventually died, and a daughter, Blanche. Blanche married a Scottish lord who was in need of money – lots of it. He also dabbled in portrait painting and had a fondness for mistresses. Blanche, distressed by the mistresses, eventually took back control of her money, became a much-admired patron of the arts, collected Fra Angelico altarpieces, and divorced her husband after he had given her two daughters: my grandmother Euphemia and my great aunt Helen. Both women were committed Christians and, to the consternation of their mother Blanche, became Church of England missionaries. Helen hurried off to China and Euphemia went to work in the notorious slums of the East End of London where she eventually met my grandfather, the Rev. Selby Henrey, who had recently been ordained and had been given a junior assignment in a slum parish full of un-churched dockworkers.

My father, inevitably, ended up with an above average number of religious genes but he had his own way of dealing with them. He was not much of a churchgoer, reckoning he had been to enough church services during his youth to last a lifetime. So my first serious contact with churchgoing was daily compulsory chapel attendance at my school Northaw. It felt somewhat strange to me, although I remember with pleasure reading passages from the bible whenever it was my turn to do so. I was, thanks to my father, familiar with the bible. He considered the King James version to be one of the finest examples of English literature and was deeply attached to it. In his quixotic attempts to teach me at home, he often used the bible as a school text. I remember being made to copy psalms and parables into an exercise book, a long-drawn out process that involved lecturing mingled with scolding and, on my side, ample tears and snivelling. As far as my father was concerned faith was inextricably wound up with culture.

My mother also had strongly-held religious views. As a child she lived in Clichy, one of Paris's working-class suburbs and 'mission territory' for the French Reformed Church. She attended the mission school, not out of religious conviction – my beloved French grandmother was nominally a Catholic – but because it was free and had a good reputation. Mother and daughter were treated with respect and kindness and from then on my mother thought of herself as a Protestant. When years later my father took the bold step of introducing his attractive young girlfriend to his parents at the vicarage it must have helped that she at least had one redeeming quality; she knew her bible and was not a Papist. My mother never grew tired of saying that her Protestantism must have gone some way toward offsetting her obvious handicaps, namely that she was foreign, spoke halting English, was penniless and had little schooling beyond the elementary grades..

I was expected to say my prayers every night kneeling beside my bed and to attempt to keep my tears in check when made to copy out psalms and parables. My father had very little interest in science and thus no sympathy for people who went around saying that it had taken more than six days to create the world. My mother, who had strong views on all kinds of subjects and expressed them freely, was somewhat scornful of Catholics – regarding them as unthinking and somewhat superstitious in religious matters.

So even though my parents rarely, if ever, went to church, religion was part of the landscape, and the idea of my attending a Catholic school therefore turned out to be no trifling matter. I do not think it would have happened had my paternal grandmother been alive. She had objected some years earlier to my father agreeing to my acting in *The Fallen Idol*. The film's success, the unexpected amount of press coverage, and the visibility of the child's role in the telling of the story had, if anything, made matters worse. My father had weathered the storm but my sense is that it did, to a degree, affect his relationship with his mother. His younger sister, my aunt Blanche, had never married and had stayed home ostensibly to care for her ageing parents. She was fair-haired, blue eyed and heavyset. She had also inherited her father's attachment to Victorian values – without, though, his stern demeanour. By her lights, her brother was a free spirited eccentric whose erratic behaviour invariably put him at odds with the rest of the family. She was not exactly my father's advocate.

My father's older sister, Aunt Kitty, was far more forgiving of his eccentricities. She had inherited many of her mother's traits, her sharp intellect, her piercing dark eyes, high cheekbones, and her interest in religion. She taught herself Arabic, was strongly aware and proud of her Jewish ancestry, and spent a good many years in Syria and Lebanon, overtly as a member of a Christian bible society, but in practice much more committed to the challenge of earning the trust of her many Islamic friends. I have no reason to believe she ever gave my acting career more than a passing thought. I had, and still do have, a great affinity for Aunt Kitty.

Then there was my great aunt Helen – the one who had spent her youth as a missionary in Southern China. She had, late in life and well past childbearing age, married a Scottish preacher by the name of George Ramsey and, with her share of what was left of the Rothschild inheritance, helped found what would probably be referred to today as an evangelical church. She had thus provided a pulpit for the man who became known in our family as Uncle George, or George for short. My father, as a sign of his utter contempt for the man, would refer to the cockroaches that each night crawled out of the innards of our Mayfair flat and invaded the kitchen as *Georges*, pronounced the French way as in Georges Clémenceau. They were indomitable creatures and I remember my surprise when one day I learned that normal people referred to them as cockroaches rather than by the given name of the man who had married my great aunt Helen. It goes without saying that the mere mention of my film career within the Ramsey household was sufficient, at least according to my parents' recounting of the matter, to unleash tumbrels of fire and brimstone.

The Ramseys lived in East Anglia somewhere between Norwich and Cambridge and I remember being sent away to pay them a visit. It must have been some kind of peace mission imposed on my father for the greater good of the family since Aunt Helen was sick to the point of being close to death. I was, after all, the only member of the family who belonged to the next generation; extinction was a very real possibility. In yet another surprise, I was treated with kindness and consideration and to this day remember a visit to Norwich where the good-natured woman who nursed my great aunt treated me to a guided tour of the oubliettes and torture chambers of the mediaeval castle – not a fancy my parents would have indulged me in, but something I found greatly appealing. I have, however, no doubt that Aunt Helen and Uncle George would have viewed with righteous horror anything even remotely connected with Popish practices.

It is therefore with some trepidation that at the age of 13 I was sent off to Somerset to my new school, Downside. In a custom that seemed the very essence of British boarding school life, and is even referred to in the Harry Potter saga, children were brought by parents to a designated London station to catch the so-called school train. I remember being handed over at Paddington Station, which was grimy and damp, it still being the age of the steam engine, to my new fate, a total stranger in the midst of unfamiliar faces. I would not see my parents again for several months and I felt thoroughly uprooted, exiled as I was from Normandy, from my grandmother, from her cats and her chickens and from all the familiar objects that surrounded the ancient farmhouse.

The new school was, I suppose, an improvement over the old one. I was a little older, and I now had some idea of what life was like in a boarding school. It was, however, still a draughty place full of strangers, full of rules and constraints. In winter we were made to get up before dawn and wash in the cold. The food was soggy and bland – potatoes, fried bread, institutional scrambled egg, green beans turned blue and mushy from overcooking, token slices of flabby grey tinged meat and for pudding, sponge-like yellow cake soaked in viscous syrup. We were still living in the aftermath of the war, or so we were told, and that was just the way food came.

We wore black ties, white shirts – with stiff finger-bruising starched collars that, for the sake of cleanliness, had to be changed every second day – black jackets and pin-striped pants. This elaborate gear was subject to much smudging and staining, and not just from ink from leaky pens. When unsupervised we threw food at each other and when we got into fights – also when unsupervised – were not supposed to pull on each other's ties but we did, stretching them and crushing them miserably.

In the afternoon we played rugby, cricket or field hockey, depending on the season, and wore shirts sporting the colours of the house to which we were assigned. My house was Smythe and my shirts were striped orange and black, generally muddy, and often torn. For some reason there were never enough boots to go around, and to survive we kept those we owned under lock and key. Punishments were meted out to those who showed up to a game bootless. The same rules applied to boot laces. Socks, however, were in more plentiful supply. The idea behind all this hassle was, I suppose, to teach us that fairness has no lasting role in human affairs and that survival is an everyday imperative. Perhaps, but it could also be that there was no particular purpose to any of this and that this was simply the way life was.

We slept in dormitories – large rooms with high ceilings – that were poorly heated and dimly lit. Beds were lined up in neat rows. Beside each bed was a small cupboard where we kept our laundered clothes together with a metal mug for washing and drinking. Each one of our possessions, down to our handkerchiefs, toothbrushes and mugs, was numbered. Mine was 55 and it remained with me throughout my school career. It was very much part of each person's identity. The British institutional system discouraged the use of first names – only surnames could be used. Where there were several boys with the same name, it was essential to tell them apart with numbers. Toward the end of my school career a couple of brothers showed up whose surname was Henry. Even though they spelt their name without an 'e', I became Henrey 1, and they 2 and 3 respectively.

The beds were heavy iron-framed contraptions strung with a crisscross of wires that supported skinny, unyielding and much-stained mattresses. Dormitories were places for sleeping only: there was no talking, no reading and no socialising. Bathrooms were austere and communal. We stood on wooden slatted boards and faced long rows of basins, showers and toilets. There was a time and a place for everything; a quarter of an hour to wash and dress in the morning and, in the evening, ten minutes to prepare for bed. Some of the older boys had the job of enforcing discipline. They were given the title of prefect – in imitation, I suppose, of the hierarchical system that sustained the Roman Empire over so many centuries. The most usual form of punishment was the assignment of something called blue paper. A prefect could assign one or two pages depending on the seriousness of the breach of discipline. The paper was lined and we were obliged to cover it back and front with handwriting. It was meant to be repetitious, boring and time consuming. A phrase such as 'I am being punished for talking between classes' might have to be copied over and over again. If no such phrase was assigned it was acceptable to write a free-form essay: a far less burdensome chore but one that was not without risk. I, for one, could not always resist the temptation of trying my hand at writing a deliberately one-sided and highly fanciful account of the incident that had given rise to the punishment. That was dangerous because it inevitably degenerated into satire and criticism of authority. The risk, of course, was that the prefect who had assigned the blue paper, and to whom it had to be returned within 48 hours, might actually read it. If he lacked a well-developed sense of humour the consequences could be quite disagreeable. The blue paper system in fact incorporated a devilish catch.

The upper school was divided into four houses, each incorporating some 80 boys of all ages. Dormitories, bathrooms and various other facilities such as recreation areas were grouped by house. The names given to each of the four houses were those of men who were part of the school's Benedictine history.

One was a bishop who at the beginning of the 17th century had established the original monastery at Douai in northern France as a foundation for exiled English monks. Two others, Saint Ambrose Barlow and Saint John Roberts were priests from that same monastery who, flouting anti-Catholic laws, had ministered in England and suffered execution. The fourth was an English aristocrat who, in a strange reversal of political correctness, had been allowed by the English crown to welcome into his Shropshire estate the Douai monks who had been dispossessed and imprisoned during the French Revolution. This was a time when the English establishment worried more about anti-royalist mobs than about the potentially corrosive influence of Popish monks.

I was at the time blissfully unaware of this rich and convoluted history. All I knew was that my house was Smythe and that our rivals, believing that we owed our name to a Mr Smith who out of vainglory had gentrified his name by substituting a 'y' for an 'i' and adding an 'e', taunted us by referring to us as barbarians from Smith House. It was, in fact, named after Sir Edward Smythe who had welcomed the fugitive monks into his Shropshire house in 1795.

Each house had a housemaster. Mine was a kindly monk who went by the name of Dom Ceolfrid. Why such a strange name? The Dom part was easy enough to explain: it was a contraction of the Latin *Dominus*, or Sir, by which Benedictines have, over the centuries, referred to themselves. Well and good, but what about Ceolfrid? Neither I nor anyone else in Smythe had the slightest idea. We did know that when monks were professed they took on new names but beyond that we just accepted the name as yet another of the cultural oddities that surrounded us. I had indeed been parachuted into a world that bore absolutely no resemblance to anything I had previously experienced. Today, over a half-century later, I have access to the magic of Google. According to Wikipedia, Ceolfrid was a 7th century Anglo-Saxon abbot who had a great love for books and is reputed to have amassed 300 volumes; at the time by far the largest library in all of England. Now that I have reached a ripe old age, I delight in such trivia.

Dom Ceolfrid was a tall, gaunt, ascetic looking man with piercing eyes, a prominent nose and a long muscular face. While on duty he always wore his habit – a simple black robe with a folded back hood. One of the things I liked about Dom Ceolfrid was that he kept a kennel full of beagles – hare hunting hounds. The kennels were hidden behind the monastic gardens and there was something excitingly un-monkish about the way he cared for his dogs. In addition to vows of chastity, Benedictines take vows of poverty and obedience to their abbot. But there was absolutely no question that the beagles belonged to Dom Ceolfrid. There was no knowing what kind of arrangement he had worked out with the abbot, however I now suspect that abbots are elected by their fellow monks to their high office based on their willingness to put up with the foibles and eccentricities of those over whom they hold sway. Dom Ceolfrid clearly needed his beagles and, notwithstanding the Rule of Saint Benedict, they were his dogs. I was no great dog lover – these beagles were in a class apart from my mother's Pekingese – and Normandy is not hare hunting country, but there was something very special about the beagles. They needed regular exercise, and they provided me with an opportunity to run with them on afternoons when, according to school rules, I should have been playing rugby, cricket or field hockey. Dom Ceolfrid must have known that there were boys within his charge who occasionally needed to be let off the hook when it came to playing games.

There was a problem with this blue paper business. The school shop that sold stationery and sweets was not an authorised supplier. Only housemasters could give it out. Dom Ceolfrid had a small office close to the cavernous dormitories that were assigned to Smythe House. Those of us needing to see him were expected to line up outside his office during the morning hour set aside for recreation; a recreation during which we were expected to bulk up with a Government-issued half pint of milk and a sticky, spongy yellow bun sporting the occasional raisin.

There were favours to be asked and problems to be attended to. Father Ceolfrid was also our banker. At the beginning of each school term we were required to hand over whatever pocket money our parents had given us. The sums, not just according to the school rules but also by economic necessity, were paltry; £5 to last the several months of a term would have been pushing the limits of propriety. We did, however, need money for sweets, for purchasing pens from the school shop and for making phone calls home from an ancient machine with two clunky buttons. The person at the other end could not hear a thing until button A had been pressed – it was then that the machine noisily swallowed whatever pennies, sixpences, and shillings had been inserted into the slot – and B was for refunds in the event of an unanswered call. Father Ceolfrid kept our individual accounts in a large leather bound ledger. Each of our withdrawals – however trifling – was accounted for. That ledger, however, had a more sinister purpose. It was also used to tally exactly how many pages of blue paper had been given out to each of us. It was a bit like the ledger in which the Almighty is reputed to make careful note of each of our transgressions and to which he then refers on the Day of Judgment. There was a limit to the accumulation of these pages of blue - three or four handed out over a period of a couple of weeks might be testing the limits. Father Ceolfrid might then, instead of handing out the requested page of blue, ask the victim to close the door - a dreaded preamble of things to come - pull out a shiny bamboo cane from behind his desk, require a bending over, and then administer four or six strokes in quick succession. Father Ceolfrid had a reputation for fairness and no one ever suggested that he took pleasure in any of this but he was a strong man and fit from exercising his beagles. There is no denying that this caning business was painful. It was also humiliating since there was always a long line of boys outside his office. They would count the strokes and comment on the perceived intensity of each whack. Since I was neither boastful nor reckless and somewhat shy by nature, I managed to keep my pages of blue within acceptable limits and receive fewer whacks than most.

Then there was the business of religion. Remarkably, I was the only non-Catholic in the school. It had been made quite clear to me that I would be treated no differently than anyone else. I was expected to attend services and there were plenty of them. There was early morning Mass three days a week and on Sundays a mid-morning High Mass, preceded by the monastic hours of Terce and Sext, and then Vespers in the evening. There were other devotions thrown in such as Benediction on Fridays followed by Compline. I had been warned about things like incense and bells, and the tendency of Catholics to genuflect - to make the sign of the cross - sometimes quite unpredictably, and to sprinkle water around. It was indeed all very strange but not in any threatening way. The fact is that no one expected me to do anything in particular. I was teased for plenty of things - including, of course, inevitably *The Fallen Idol* - but never for not being a Catholic: I suspect that some of the boys might even have been envious of me for having one less thing to worry about. Some of the things I witnessed were stranger to me than others. I marvelled at the way in which boys lined up to go to confession. Confession was available before every weekday mass, right up to the consecration that in those days was followed by a jangle of bells. There were a number of confessionals lined up along one of the side aisles. These unadorned, unvarnished, big pine rectangular boxes seemed incongruous in the midst of the neo-Gothic splendour of the abbey church. These were quickie confessions. I could not help noticing that no one spent much time inside the boxes – except, of course, for the priests whose job it was to hear the boys' confessions. What was this all about? Some of my classmates obligingly filled me in on the theological concept of mortal sin. If a boy wanted to receive Holy Communion at a morning weekday mass he had to be free of mortal sin. So? Well, my mentors explained, masturbation was a big problem. One of the confessors – my recollection was that he went by the name of Father Leander and that he was both Irish and white-haired – enjoyed a particularly fine reputation: he was understanding and remarkably expeditious. The lines beside his big pine box were by far the longest but they moved mercifully quickly.

One of the monks took pity on me and gave me a large leather-bound missal he had found in the bottom of a drawer. It included the scriptural readings for weekday as well as for Sunday masses in both French and Latin. "A good way to keep up your French and practise your Latin," he said to me. "You'll find it a lot more interesting than Caesar's Gallic military campaigns and that way you'll avoid being bored in church." This wise man was a poet and one of Father Ceolfrid's friends – a friend to the point of occasionally showing up to help exercise the beagles. He was right. I started looking forward to the quietness of church. It marked the beginning of my intellectual awakening – there was pleasure indeed in studying something at my own pace and without being accountable to anyone else.

9

The End Of Schooling

My life was split between two quite separate worlds. The small Mayfair flat was no place for me to stay. It really never had been, but its unsuitability became all the more apparent as I moved into my teenage years. My parents – individualistic and self-sufficient as ever – had not thought it necessary to make the effort required to belong to a network of social acquaintances. This meant that, outside of school, I had few opportunities to develop friendships with people of my own age. At the end of each school term there was nothing for me to do but return to Normandy.

I was, as it happened, perfectly happy to do so. The ancient farmhouse was, in a sense, the only home I had known and my relationship with my grandmother was as close as ever. In Normandy I did have friends of my own age. They were the sons of neighbours and farmers for the most part. Life in post-war France remained frugal. Few families had cars and the only practical way of getting around was on a bike – even mopeds were considered a luxury. My friends had by now finished their formal schooling and were learning trades. I enjoyed their company. I too would have enjoyed learning carpentry or plumbing or electricity. I had a fair idea of what they were up to and, in some ways, envied them. But what I could not even begin to do was adequately describe to them the makeup of the other half of my own life: the life I was expected to lead the moment I stepped off the boat in England, just in time to begin yet another school term.

On Sundays in France we would meet up and go bike riding. I had seen enough of the world to know that this part of Normandy was exceptionally beautiful, but we were no tourists. We rode our bikes down country lanes in search of freedom. We bought our lunch in the villages; baguettes from the baker, ham from the pork butcher, and beer from the grocer. The beer came in large reusable bottles with old-fashioned stoppers – the kind that were made of glazed vitreous china, had a bright orange rubber removable seal and were held tightly in place with a pushdown metal clasp. I had never drunk beer at home; this was freedom, indeed. We were old enough to be interested in girls. My friends were still too young to have regular girlfriends – this was rural Europe in the 1950s – but they at least had their sights on the local girls. I wished I had been so lucky. We spoke in hushed tones and passed around girly magazines – nothing glossy and nothing too explicit – again this was the 1950s.

My grandmother was good at not asking me too many questions. She was as happy to have me to herself as I was to be away from school and from my parents. We talked endlessly. I was growing up and she was able to share more of herself. Her rheumatic pain was increasingly hard to bear. I wished it had been otherwise, but I still suffered from the self-centredness of youth and was a poor listener. Her doctor had begun to prescribe steroids. They worked well, particularly at the beginning, but they turned out to be no miracle cure; especially since their dangerous side effects were as yet poorly understood. She made no bones about having had a hard life and spoke openly about her disappointments. The fact that my parents had written and published a book about her without so much as asking her permission rankled her. They had called it *Matilda and the Chickens.* She was mortified. She was shy about her name feeling that it was old-fashioned. I, of course, sided with her: I always had. She never talked to me about the death of her two-year old son Robert. I now wish she had but I also understand that she was wise not to attempt to share such deep pain with a person as young as I then was. She continued to look after her hens and rabbits, and care for the cats and for my mother's Pekingese Pouffy. As a child she had lived beside the Loire. The hens and the rabbits must have connected her with her childhood. It had, from what she told me, been a happy one.

It was largely thanks to my grandmother that the essence of who I was began to take root within the soil around the old farmhouse; a powerful feeling that this was my home and the place to which I would always return, regardless of how far afield I wandered. There was a paradox here because I was, at the very same time, being shaped within the mould of an upper class English education; shaped perhaps, trimmed and even nurtured, but this rooting business was not something to be ignored.

Through force of habit the strangeness of school gradually wore off. I began to make friends, I was at last in a place where few people seemed to know or care much that I had been a film star – that was a huge relief – and I began to take more of an interest in what I was being taught in class. There was a reason for that.

Downside had, in those years, acquired a reputation for academic excellence in very large part due to the hard-driving personality of its then headmaster. Dom Wilfrid was tall, overweight to the point of possessing a stomach that bulged conspicuously under the tent-like folds of his oversize black Benedictine habit. His brow sweated profusely, his short-cropped hair bristled and his eyes darted back and forth behind thick lenses perched precariously on the tip of his huge nose. No one trifled with Father Wilfrid; this bear of a man looked more like a heavyweight boxer than a headmaster. It was he who had acceded to the request of my mother's friend that I be considered for admission to the school even though no one in my family had ever had the slightest connection with the Benedictines, let alone with the Catholic religion. He worked like a demon – in today's world he would be referred to as a chronic workaholic – had a passion for scholarship and made no bones of the fact that he had very little interest in sports: all this notwithstanding the pride of place invariably given to organised sports within the British boarding school system. Father Wilfrid supervised the academic progress of each of the more than 300 boys in the school – he was all seeing and relentless.

At the end of my first year in school, Father Wilfrid summoned me. He was in the habit of standing in the corridor just outside his office and dealing with us one by one, meting out justice and dispensing advice to whoever had reached the head of the line. It was fast and efficient and generally safer than being invited inside since such visits all too often ended in a caning. Those who were summoned had their names scrawled on a scrap of paper tacked to the notice board in the assembly hall. He greeted me with the observation that the time had now come for me to prove that his admitting me to the school had not been a mistake. "We are going to make you excel in what you already do well," he said to me. He prescribed English essay writing, an intensive course in French literature and beginner Spanish. For everything else I was placed in remedial classes. He made it clear he expected As for the English, the French and the Spanish, and simple passes for everything else. He had me all figured out. I often needed extra time to think things through but there was, according to him, a reason for that. I was slow at assimilating facts for the good reason that my mind was busy working on ideas. That was fine. Those who actually had ideas needed to treat them with respect and give them free rein. It was the school's job to make sure that ideas got plenty of attention. He was a superb diagnostician. I remember so clearly being in that corridor hearing those wise words. The others in the line behind were in no mood to eavesdrop; they were just hoping that they had not been summoned to account for some misdeed that might end in a few thwacks of Father Wilfrid's cane.

I had also grown more familiar with the pervasive influence of monasticism over school life. The monastic bells rang throughout the day: for prime, for the daily community mass, for vespers, for compline and for meals. The monks lived apart from the school and yet they were always present, mingling with the lay teachers and then, at set times, we were invited into the abbey church so we could hear mass and listen to the chanting of the offices. I was curious by nature and, having been brought up as an only child in contact with adults, was used to asking questions. I found myself asking more and more.

There was a certain Father Meinrad who was part of the small group of monks who took refuge from the rigours of the Rule of Saint Benedict by caring for Father Ceolfrid's beagles. Even though he had taken on the name of a 9th century Swiss hermit, he was Irish and had a reputation for being a little strange. Part of the strangeness had to do with his speaking with a pleasant, but decidedly unusual, high-pitched, almost soulful, intonation. He also had a prodigious memory: especially for lists of numbers and timetables. He could, at a moment's notice, recite the times of departure and arrival of trains for each of the stations between Wells and Bath. Strange indeed, especially since there was no obvious reason why he should ever have the need to take the train. The other thing about Father Meinrad is that he was mechanically minded and had managed to put together an impressive collection of metal and woodworking tools. He stored his lathes, drills and presses in a shed not far from Father Ceolfrid's kennels. Even though the abbot must have known about the shed – just as he could not help knowing about the beagles – it was an exciting place to visit since it had all the fascination of a forbidden garden. Speaking of forbidden gardens, Father Meinrad was an excellent biblical scholar and stood ready to expound at great length on any theological subject, including, of course, original sin. The shed was a good place to ask questions because he also stored within it an impressive collection of theological and reference books.

As I was approaching my 16th birthday, I woke up one day with an awareness of how much I had changed over the past few years. I had acquired a taste for knowledge and was learning things that I actually wanted to know about and in ways that were appealing to me. I was, at last, making choices for myself. I had, in the past, achieved fame as a child actor but the fame had not come to me as a result of something I had chosen. It felt almost as if I had been subjected to an experience others had caused to happen. Perhaps that was why I had unconsciously tried so very hard to distance myself from the filmmaking episode of my early life. It was not something I had chosen to do and so, in a sense, it did not count as a personal achievement. That might be why the whole business of having been a child star had caused me such embarrassment and confusion.

The suggestion that I learn Spanish turned out to be a good one. I had stumbled at first, but had then fallen in love with the language. No one in my family had ever learned Spanish, so this was something I was doing for myself. The more I read in Spanish the more excitement I derived from glimpsing into a culture that was totally new to me. I tackled poems by Teresa of Ávila on the inside of my locker door and began to read Don Quixote. I did earn As in the subjects prescribed by Father Wilfrid and just about managed a passing grade in everything else.

One unintended consequence of all this was that I decided to become a Catholic. I had grown accustomed to the monks chanting the monastic hours and there was something grounding about the recitation of the psalms in Latin and the tones of Gregorian chant. It was a decision that had perhaps much more to do with my search for cultural identity than with the acceptance of a particular set of beliefs. The ritual seemed to respond to a side of my personality that needed a safe and harmonious space within which to reflect and to experience emotions. I had also gradually grown used to the culture of Catholicism: the emphasis on sacramental communion, the succession of saints' days, the quaintness of its traditions and its willingness to assimilate and even tolerate popular beliefs. These things seemed to fit within my own cultural framework, particularly my French roots, and my growing interest in the Hispanic world.

My mother greeted the news with dismay – less so my father. My father's way of asserting his independence as a young man was to escape from Oxford after barely of year of desultory study and go on a long trip. His mother probably gave him just about enough money to buy himself a berth on a transatlantic steamer but the fact is that he needed a job. He ended up in Quebec and started working as a very junior reporter for local newspapers; he always claimed that journalism was in his blood. My father fell in love with Quebec and Catholicism in those days was very much part of the French Canadian identity. He was a great admirer of all things picturesque and the colourfulness of religious practice in Quebec struck him as refreshingly different from the austerity of the suburban London vicarage of his youth. My decision would have given him far more pause for concern had his parents been alive but the fact is that they were long dead. He was also realistic about the fact that while he had done his best to pass on to me his reverence for the 16th century English of the King James Bible, he had not done much else when it came to religion. Had it not been for my mother, he would probably not have given the matter a second thought.

My mother, of course, saw things quite differently. By marrying my father, she had made England her adopted home and therefore had every reason to identify with Protestantism. She was wary of Catholicism, despised it for its association with the smugness of the French bourgeoisie and considered many of its practices as superstitious. Sparks flew, particularly since my mother was outspoken and inclined to be scathingly critical of those with whom she took issue. She reacted angrily and berated me for my lack of good sense but by then I knew better. I even had an inkling that my decision was in large measure related to a need for me to assert my own independence.

My French grandmother, with whom I still felt very close, had the good sense to keep her opinions largely to herself. She had her own reasons for being attached to the biblically rooted faith she had been exposed to by the Protestant missionaries in the slums of Paris but she was also inclined to side with me; especially against my mother. I was increasingly aware of the complex emotional intensity underlying the love hate relationship between mother and daughter.

As I approached my 17th birthday, my father began to worry about what I was going to do for a living. He kept hoping against hope that I would follow in his footsteps and become a journalist. This is something he felt surprisingly strongly about and he enlisted my mother's support. Why not leave school as quickly as possible and take an entry-level job in a newspaper? My father had equally strong ideas about the need to earn cash. I would, he assured me, be thrilled to earn my first pay packet. He waxed lyrical about the little brown envelope that would come my way every couple of weeks containing a few pounds, some silver coins, and maybe pennies. I listened politely but remained unconvinced and referred my problem to Father Wilfrid. "Nonsense!" he said to me no sooner had I reached the head of the line outside his office. "I'll make sure you get into university."

The End Of Schooling

Getting into university, as Father Wilfrid put it, in Britain in the 1950s was a difficult and chancy business. Two factors had conspired to make entry into universities hugely competitive. Socially conscious post war governments had spent large sums of money improving the quality of teaching in state secondary schools. There was an understandable desire to make Britain more competitive by greatly increasing what had until then been the woefully small number of students prepared to pursue higher education. Government policy was aimed at opening up universities to students of ability, regardless of social background, and thereby doing away with the unfair advantages enjoyed by the privately run public schools. The only problem was that far less government money had been spent on expanding existing universities and next-to-nothing on creating new ones.

This was a situation that clearly stimulated Father Wilfrid's love of competition and so I was added to the group of boys selected for academic overdrive. University education in those days was a highly academic and specialised pursuit. Each candidate was examined in the subject he or she proposed to study and the system allowed for very little flexibility. I would be expected to demonstrate that, in addition to mastering English essay writing, I could write decently in both Spanish and French and that I had a fair knowledge of both literary traditions. For me all this was a stretch.

I spent my next summer in Normandy surrounded by books. The days of long bike rides with my old friends, talking about girls and sipping beer, were over. It was not just the fault of my books. We had drifted apart in other respects. France was in the midst of fighting an increasingly bloody and utterly confusing war in Algeria and my friends were waiting to be drafted into the army. They were a year or so older than I so now had steady girlfriends. It was not unusual for the girl to get pregnant just before the time due for the beginning of the man's military service. In those days it was customary to make things right by marrying a few days before beginning basic training. I was living in a different world to theirs. There were no girls on my horizon and it had been assumed I would be granted an educational deferment from military service.

My grandmother watched over me as I read endless books: the poets and playwrights of the court of Louis XIV and of the masters of the Spanish Golden Age. The chickens and the cats were still there but she had given up the rabbits: her days of going out in the field to hand pick choice grasses and dandelion leaves had come to an end: the arthritis had got the better of her. She still cooked, though, and I still cycled down the hill every morning to buy the meat and groceries for the day. I was grateful that not everything in my life had changed. I still slept in the little room upstairs with the half-timbering and the ill-fitting little window from which I could watch the cows munching at the grass in the field beyond the garden fence.

In early December 1956, age 17, the school taxi took me to Bath and I caught a train for Oxford. When I got off the train I realised the station was swarming with candidates and that the students were on their Christmas break. I remember the pungent smell of soot-laden smoke as the fog settled gently in the midst of the cooling night air. Father Wilfrid had selected a college for me: Lincoln – one that offered several places for candidates interested in studying languages.

The college porter called me *Sir,* took my bag and led me to a room in one of the Gothic buildings located in the far quadrangle. All I knew was that in the morning I was expected to show up for breakfast in the dining hall. I had purchased an alarm clock for that very purpose for the princely sum of 21 shillings. It was a big round German made contraption with luminous hands surmounted with a tough-looking bell. Rooms in Oxford colleges were generally arranged around numbered staircases rather than floors. Each staircase was fitted with a couple of toilets and urinals for the common use of its residents, but beyond that there was no plumbing. Nor was there any central heating. Instead, each room had a gas fire; a cast-iron museum piece fitted with a latticed ceramic front up which hissed blue-yellow flames. I had been told to bring a supply of shilling coins. The shillings went into a slot that fed the gas meter beside the fire.

In the morning a large, stooped, elderly man walked into my room carrying a jug of water. Rooms had double doors but no locks; to shut the outer one was referred to as 'sporting one's oak' and a sign that visitors were unwelcome. The water was for shaving and he placed it on a washstand; a piece of Victorian furniture large enough to accommodate a heavy white enamelled basin. Beneath was a bucket for the soapy swill. Victorians must have lived this way and considered it progress. I need not have invested in the German alarm clock because the man greeted me with a grunt-like good morning and called me Sir; just like the hall porter the previous evening. I later learned that he was responsible for keeping tidy the rooms on his staircase. Oxford colleges still had servants – menservants of course – keeping alive the tradition that students were gentlemen entitled to the privileges of their class. College servants were called scouts. Why so, I had no idea but I just assumed their title was as old as the college itself. While by no means the oldest of Oxford's more than 20 colleges, this particular one was nonetheless mediaeval – founded a few years before the fall of Constantinople – and endowed by the Bishop of Lincoln for young men from his diocese; especially those who felt called to clerical life. In those days any man connected with an Oxford college was expected to be celibate. This was a tradition that endured until Victorian times and still imparted a monastic-like feeling to the place.

The dining hall was a grand place with a high vaulted ceiling held up by honest-to-goodness Gothic arches. The arched windows were fitted with stained glass and the walls panelled with oak that had been darkened by centuries of polishing. We the candidates sat on benches on both sides of rows of massive tables that were probably as ancient as the panels. We sat awkwardly, complete strangers to each other, wearing somewhat self-consciously the dull coloured and frumpy uniforms of our respective schools. After breakfast, the tables were cleared and we were invited to begin the first three-hour examination of the day. Each of us was given a set of questions corresponding to the academic discipline in which we had chosen to be examined. Among us were mathematicians, chemists, classicists, historians, physicists, political theorists and a host of other aspiring scholars. We took out our pens and set to work. In those days ballpoints were prone to smudge and not considered worthy of the task at hand. Instead, we used fountain pens that were equally unreliable and leaky but were held in esteem because of their gold-tipped nibs. There were altogether too many of us so we rubbed shoulders awkwardly. At the end of the morning session, scouts appeared to serve us lunch. Dinner was no different, it followed the afternoon examination session and we ate and worked, each at his appointed place, at the tables we had chanced to sit for breakfast on the first morning. So far as I can remember, the whole business stretched out over some three days and at one point I was summoned into a large room with a gilded ceiling for an interview by a group of dons sitting behind a long table. I remember it as a quite formal but not particularly threatening affair – certainly no stranger than everything else about those three extraordinary days.

After dinner, though, the candidates were let loose on the town. There were others from my school who, just like me, had came to Oxford and were competing for places at colleges all over town. We met in pubs, drank beer and smoked a cigarette or two. There was probably a minimum legal age for drinking in a pub but it did not seem to apply to students. We joked and commiserated with one another right up to closing time. Pubs were friendly, smoke-filled places that reeked of warm bitter beer and sheltered us from the cold. December in Oxford is a foggy, damp month and the streets around the colleges are for the most part narrow and ill lit. I remember walking back from the pub to my staircase and hearing a succession of church bells strike out the hour. It was then that I decided that I really wanted to come there.

Luckily for me, just after Christmas, the college sent a brief letter to Father Wilfrid, informing him that I was among those chosen. Whenever I hear church bells striking or pealing on a misty, damp-smelling winter evening, I relive that nostalgic moment.

10

Oxford

A couple of obstacles still stood in the way of my going to Oxford. I had two nationalities: one inherited from my father who was British-born and the other arising out of my French birth. In the 1950s the Cold War was very much a reality so that the British were still drafting men for compulsory military services. Oxford colleges had so few places to give out that they routinely set as a condition of admission a two-year waiting time; long enough for a man to fulfill that obligation. The British government was at the same time running out of money. Taxes were impossibly burdensome and spending on social programmes was on the rise. I was in good health but excessively near-sighted. That, under the circumstances, was reason enough to exempt me from National Service.

The French, on the other hand, were fighting one of the nastiest wars in their history in Algeria, and could not have cared less about my nearsightedness. On my 18th birthday two gendarmes visited me. They came down the field in full uniform and kepis, their caps with horizontal peaks, wheeling their bikes along the muddy drive. Friendly to the point of being apologetic, they nonetheless handed me a train ticket together with a summons to appear at a military base somewhere in far-away Brittany. This was a brush with cold reality. Even though I had begun to take a strong interest in politics – France was living through the chaos that would eventually persuade General De Gaulle to abandon his self-imposed retirement and return to the rescue – I had absolutely no desire to be drafted into service in Algeria. Besides, being from a non-military family and having few of the physical and psychological attributes required for successful soldiering, I felt woefully unprepared. One of the military attachés in the French Consulate in London fortunately took up my case and I was eventually granted an exemption – once again my excessive short-sightedness was taken into account. In the process the college that had admitted me agreed to reduce my waiting period from two years to one.

How, though, was I to spend this in-between year? This was 1957 and the idea of taking a year off to explore the world – the gap year that has become such a part of the worldwide youth scene – was simply not on the cards. My father would have liked me to take a job but even that idea proved impractical. The pittance I might have earned would have barely covered my rent. There was certainly no room for me in the Mayfair flat for it was still the overheated cubbyhole my parents had moved into at the beginning of the war, almost two decades earlier.

So I stayed put in Normandy with my grandmother. It really was the one place I could call home. Initially, it felt strangely different. For years now I had kissed my grandmother goodbye at the end of the summer and taken the bus to Le Havre, from where I had crossed the Channel so I could go back to school. This time I stayed behind. This was before the great building boom of the 60s and 70s. In those days the Parisians on holiday packed up at the end of August and left what we still referred to as the village to the locals. It was a time for dismantling and stowing away the whitewashed wooden cabins that had lined the beach all summer long, for farming families to wade into tidal pools harvesting the fat, juicy mussels that clung to rocks so distant that only September's equinoctial tides could lay them bare, and for apples to be gathered into large heaps ready for autumnal cider making. It was also the season for smelling smoke from wood fires, for stacking logs and for taking long walks along the windswept, deserted beach. Autumn is a wonderful season, especially for the young, who only have the slightest of suspicions that it is also a harbinger of decay and death.

My old friends, the ones with whom I had spent Sunday afternoons cycling and chortling over girlie magazines, had moved away so that there was no one around of my own age. There was, however, Patsy. In those days, she and her husband Jacques rented a large, rambling house half a mile or so down the road at the point at which the high ground begins to fall off sharply toward the village below. Not only did their house have a magnificent view over the sea – a view that stretched across the bay of the Seine as far as Le Havre – but it was also an exceptionally friendly and welcoming place. Patsy and Jacques formed an attractive couple and they already had three children. Patsy's mother was French but her father was a British naval officer who had spent most of his career on the high seas and died in Singapore – probably of a tropical disease – shortly before the

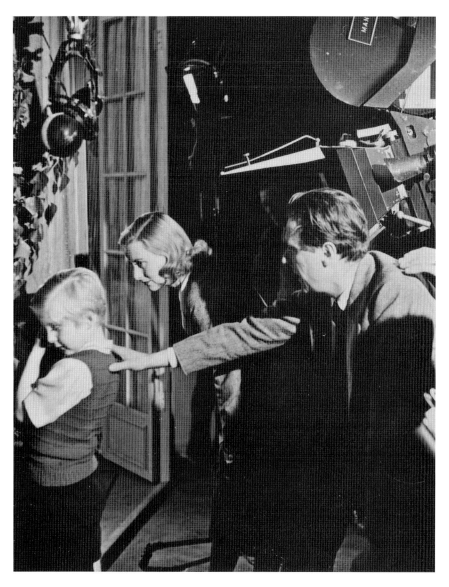

On the set of The Fallen Idol *with Michèle Morgan and director Carol Reed. In this scene I discover that Mrs Baines has found my snake McGregor and disposed of him in the basement stove!*

(*by kind permission of David Rayner*)

The famous scene in the police station with Dora Bryan. This is the studio-built police station to which I am brought after being discovered wandering the London streets in the middle of the night.

(*British Film Institute*)

One of the shots of me looking down from above at the adult world below. This is vintage Carol Reed – angled shots and bemused looks.

(*British Film Institute*)

On the set of The Fallen Idol *with Ralph Richardson.*

My mother on the set of The Fallen Idol *during filming*

A publicity photograph for The Fallen Idol *of me with Ralph Richardson, Michèle Morgan and Carol Reed.*

(*by kind permission of David Rayner*)

Presenting a bouquet of orchids to Her Majesty the Queen at the Royal Command Performance at the Empire, Leicester Square in November 1948. Ronald Reagan was also in the room! The dedication in my childish handwriting is to my father's sister, Blanche.

My mother and I at the opening night of The Fallen Idol *in 1948.*

BOBBY HENREY AS YOUNG FELIPE LOOKS WISTFULLY DOWN AT HIS IDOL, BAINES, THE EMBASSY BUTLER

DIRECTOR CAROL REED, copying one of Bobby's gestures, explains how and why he is supposed to throw out his arms helplessly in a scene from *The Fallen Idol*.

PATIENTLY EXPLAINING every last detail, Reed gets down to the boy's level and beneath it (*below*) to make every one of his gestures in the film letter-perfect.

"A STAGGERING PERFORMANCE"

London critics are bowled over by young Bobby Henrey, an Anglo-French boy whom patient direction has turned into Britain's newest child star

by FRANCIS LEVISON

LONDON

London film critics were caught off their surly guard this fall by a small boy with an uneven walk, a misbegotten haircut and an odd foreign accent. "Bobby Henrey . . . one of the most endearing child studies ever given in the cinema," "An absolutely staggering performance by an 8-year-old." "Ninety-four minutes of sheer enchantment." "Bobby Henrey . . . the incarnation of the small boy we all hope we once were."

The occasion for these rave notices was the premiere of *The Fallen Idol*, a new opus from Sir Alexander Korda's studios, which had occurred with a minimum of advance fanfare. Nobody had any business to be quite so surprised because the film was made by Carol Reed whose last, *Odd Man Out*, gave evidence of his growing into one of the world's great cinema directors. It was quite reasonable to be astonished by Bobby Henrey, however, who was billed in small letters and had never been heard of before.

Bobby Henrey, now 9 years old, is the son of a good-looking Anglo-French team of writers who commute between London and a farm in Normandy. He had never before acted in so much as a kindergarten pantomime and had not been known to perform a tap dance, sing in tune or even recite a poem with distinction.

This inexperienced boy plays the role of the ambassador's son, left alone for a weekend in a great London embassy in the care of the butler, Baines (played by Sir Ralph Richardson), whom he idolizes, and Mrs. Baines, whom he hates. The child becomes the uncomprehending pawn in the adult drama created by the butler's romance with an embassy typist, Mrs. Baines's suspicious frenzies and her eventual hysterical fall down the embassy

CONTINUED ON NEXT PAGE

105

In London with my mother at the age of 15

*With my father in France 1949 - one of the very few photographs I have of him
with me.*

outbreak of war. Patsy and her widowed mother spent the war years in Paris. At one point, mother and daughter were accused by the Gestapo of hiding downed British parachutists, arrested, and jailed. They were lucky to have survived.

Jacques ran a dry cleaning business based in Rouen he had inherited from his family. The work was not overly taxing which was just as well since, at heart, he and Patsy were intellectuals. Every available surface of their rambling house was cluttered with stacks of books. Jacques had studied chemistry and he took a genuine interest in anything to do with science, especially astronomy and nuclear physics. Patsy was an avid reader and, because of her liberal views – her sympathies clearly lay with the Socialist wing of the complex spectrum of post war French politics – had a strong affinity for writers such as Albert Camus and Jean-Paul Sartre. Patsy and Jacques also had interesting friends, many of whom came by train from Paris for long weekends. I remember in particular the many members of the Casadesus family, a clan of eccentric and charming musicians. Those who took time out to come to see Patsy seemed to be lurching from one emotional crisis to the other. It was obvious that they came to her for therapeutic nurturing.

This turned out to be one of the most unusual years of my life. Here I was living alone with my grandmother experiencing a daily routine of work, study and meditation that was almost monastic. There was a great stillness about the ancient house – sitting as it did in the middle of a field – that brought me peace and an opportunity to concentrate my mind as never before.

I slept and studied as I always had in the little room that had been mine since early childhood. It was above the kitchen, its half-timbered walls painted black and white, its floorboards rough and creaky and on moonlit nights the limestone pillars of its ancient fireplace reflected a wan, pale glow. Each morning I rose before dawn and read in the midst of the stillness. After a while I would listen for my grandmother's steps as she emerged from her little room, her slippers shuffling over the worn black and white kitchen tiles. I would hear the faint click of a glass or of a cup and then the opening and closing of doors.

Patsy and Jacques were my tutors. What was I reading, and why? I had gone through school learning virtually no science: a casualty of a system that demanded in-depth academic excellence in but a few subjects. It was Jacques who introduced me to the principles of relativity and of quantum physics. From Einstein and Max Planck we moved on to Darwin. All I knew about Darwin was that my father disapproved of him. I had once attended a class in which the teacher had mentioned that the story of the creation of the world in six days was not to be taken literally. I had quite innocently reported this to my father. I should have known better and kept this useful piece of information to myself. He forthwith wrote an angry letter to the school specifying that no child of his was be subjected to this kind of nonsense. Humans, he assured me, were not descended from apes. Anyway Jacques and Patsy updated me on Darwin, and that was something I was in great need of.

It was Patsy who, at the end of that magically reflective year, drove me in her old Citroën to the bus that would take me to Le Havre so I could cross the Channel and make my way to Oxford. As a parting gift she gave me a handsome black leather briefcase. So, she said, I would have something in which to carry my lecture notes.

What I experienced during the three years that followed was, above all, a feeling of freedom. There were of course difficulties and failures to be dealt with, and some were emotionally painful; naturally, since there is nothing easy about coming of age. The beauty of it all, though, is that none of these difficulties and failures involved other people's expectations of me. Whatever success did come my way I could, for the very first time, claim as my own. I no longer felt dependent and beholden to others: not to a skillful film director such as Carol Reed, not to a chance association with great actors like Ralph Richardson, not to following a script written by Graham Greene and not to parents who had invested so much energy into the vain enterprise of forming me into a mould of their own design.

I am well aware that there are a great many who did not experience their student days through the lens of exhilarating freedom; but I did and for that reason I came to delight in the culture that was very much part of Oxford life. I am also acutely aware that this was the late 50s and early 60s and that it was a culture that was about to change: in some ways radically. Much of its quaintness would in time be swept away but the point is that I experienced it the way it was then – and that I was left with an enduring feeling that there was something about it which would help me cope with the difficulties that, in time, would surely come my way.

Had I fully outgrown *The Fallen Idol*? Was it now no more than a distant memory? Not quite. My very first week in Oxford there was a knock at my door followed by what I took to be a strange apparition: the spitting image of Oscar Wilde kitted up with a silver-knobbed cane, a carnation in the button hole, and a bright red silken neck scarf. Would I please join the Oxford University Dramatic Society: on the spot, of course? How could I not? An actor of my distinction and repute... and would I please stop doing whatever I was doing and proceed forthwith to an audition... for a leading role no less. I don't remember the play but I think it was by Tennessee Williams and I was asked – irony of ironies – to put on a Southern accent – and I failed miserably. As a consolation prize I was offered a part in the chorus of *Oedipus at Colonus*. That was the last of my being pursued by Oscar Wilde.

We undergraduates rode around on rickety bicycles with calliper brakes, or none at all, sometimes recklessly, wore academic gowns when dining in the hall of our college, invited girls to tea in our rooms, drank sherry, went to raucous bottle parties on Saturday nights, beat the midnight curfew by climbing over walls to get back into our rooms, spent summer afternoons punting lazily up and down the river, used magnificent libraries and were extended the incredible privilege of being taught individually by tutors. It was an invitation to live inside a magic bubble. I knew it would not last forever, but I did not care; fortunately, for caring about such a thing would surely have let the magic out of the bubble.

Speaking of inviting girls to tea, my neighbour Peter Hatherley and I had rooms on the same staircase and we had met on our first day in college. While I had come to Oxford to read languages, he – rather grandly, I thought – read medicine. Within Oxford's magic bubble culture undergraduates did not study subjects but rather read them. This ancient place had its own lexicon. So that those of us who had the dubious distinction of being invited to London to a weekend dance – so we could meet eligible young ladies who, as debutantes, had been presented to the Queen – went 'down' to London for the purpose. The clear message was that from Oxford there was no place in the world which one might go 'up' to – not even London!

For Peter, reading medicine meant getting up early and cycling off to some out-of-the-way laboratory – I imagined it to be dark and cavernous – so he could try his hand at dissecting embalmed cadavers. That was impressive enough but Peter also had a flair for inviting girls for tea. Our tea-making resources were meagre; we were allowed an electric kettle and not much else. Peter had developed a knack for toasting crumpets. He held them up with a fork against the fire. The crumpets, tea, milk, butter and jam were purchased from the college buttery, located in a crypt-like vaulted basement below the kitchens. The way to the buttery was down a narrow stone circular stairway. The master of the buttery was Jack; a wiry chain-smoking retired seaman with an easygoing sense of humour. He also watched over the college's wine cellar and dispensed warm bitter to those of us who chose to lunch on the buttery's cheese and pickle sandwiches. For money we used coloured tickets taken from so-called buttery books that were charged to our account – yellow for a shilling, blue for a sixpence, and various other colours assigned to lower denominations. This, I suppose, was to foster the illusion that we undergraduates lived in a world far removed from that of ordinary mortals. It was a most enticing and pleasing illusion. The buttery must have had mediaeval roots and I had little difficulty imagining Jack in the monastic garb of a lay brother, loose fitting brown robe and all.

Oxford was mediaeval in other ways. No one had a telephone. Invitations were handwritten – few of us used typewriters – and delivered via an inter-college messenger service. Girls who came to tea could often be persuaded to accept an invitation to a party. There were plenty of parties all over Oxford, especially at weekends, and most hosts were not too fussy as to who came. Gatecrashers were generally welcome although it was de rigueur to bring a girl and a bottle of cheap wine. I rejoiced in the exciting newness of all of this – new as it was to me.

What I fell in love with, though, were Oxford's libraries. Lincoln was a small college so its library was modest, but it was a wonderful place to read in the midst of the musty smell of books, both ancient and modern. It had a decent collection of large format in quarto leather-bound 16th and 17th century volumes, and just to know they were there was enough to endow the act of reading with an aura of joyful expectation. It was a place I could retreat to, especially on a foggy winter evening, so I could re-live the delight of listening to the pealing of Oxford's many bells. Later, when I read Proust, I came to realise that listening to church bells on foggy wintry evenings was, for me, what tasting a little sponge cake baked in the shape of a pilgrim's shell had been to young Marcel. Then there was the great university library founded by a man with the improbable name of Bodley. I never bothered to find out who he was but simply imagined him to be a plump Elizabethan gentleman in breeches with bags upon bags of gold guineas to spare. In any event I am deeply grateful to him. The Bodleian's huge leather-bound catalogues, request slips and majestic reading rooms – spectacular examples of Gothic elegance – undoubtedly constitute, at least as far as I am concerned, one of the world's great wonders.

Most undergraduates paid little attention to lectures and only rarely were we expected to attend them. I therefore did most of my work in libraries. It was in the Bodleian Library that I wrote my essays, at least one a week, and more often two. Essays were an essential part of Oxford's tutorial system. My principal tutor, Donald Whitton, was a man barely 10 years my senior. I remember him as gaunt, birdlike, sallow in complexion, his long dark hair carefully smoothed back, intellectually intense and immensely engaging. I liked him from the first time I met him. He wore thick tortoiseshell glasses and, because he was unmarried and by inclination would remain so, occupied a magnificent room on the first floor of the college's first and most architecturally pleasing quadrangle. The quad walls were covered in ivy and his room was to the left of the college clock – a fine black-faced instrument with gold-brushed hands and roman numerals. He stuttered slightly and sat opposite me on an elegant, silk-upholstered Victorian settee as I read my essay. Another thing about Oxford in those days was that we undergraduates did not actually hand in our essays. We read them aloud to our tutors and subjected ourselves to their oral critique. There was no such thing as the grading of an essay, in fact no grading at all and no such thing as statistics. At the end of our stay at Oxford we were subjected to a gigantic exam – a great academic reckoning, a doomsday of sorts – and that was it.

I met my tutor every Wednesday at 5pm. By lunchtime I had done as much reading as I could or cared to do. From 1pm to a few minutes before 5pm, I wrote. This was what we undergraduates referred to as an essay crisis. I invariably lived my crisis out in the Bodleian surrounded by the books I should have read. I was developing yet another lifelong habit – working under a deadline and doing so in a public place like a library, thereby seeking a measure of protection from life's many irresistible distractions.

Oxford tutors were not in the habit of lavishing praise but at least mine listened with a degree of sympathy. His room was a great book repository: they were on the floor, stacked precariously on tables and chairs and helter-skelter in bookcases. There were interruptions to my reading. He would occasionally leap up and, with the suddenness of a bird of prey readying for the kill, make a dash for whatever book he felt moved to quote from. The quote might or might not be relevant to the subject matter of my essay. That was hardly the point. It would have been a great pity to spend one whole hour commenting on my inchoate thoughts on the poetry of Baudelaire, on the novels of Flaubert or on the sentence structure of mediaeval French. There were, surely, other things to talk about. He had a passion for language;

for the ways in which different languages, notwithstanding the great diversity of their forms, all struggle with the common task of expressing the feelings that underlie human experience. He also taught me that languages reflect cultures so that each language brings with it habits of thought that are particular to it and thus imperceptibly influence a writer's thought process.

There were other kinds of interruptions: the offer of a Black Russian cigarette – a Sobranie, as I recall – or a glass of sherry. Sherry, served in small glasses, was part of Oxford's culture. There were fine Spanish amontillados for those who could afford such luxuries, or South African varieties for those who could not. My tutor's sherry was always served from a decanter, dry, clear in the glass and altogether distinguished – at least so far as I could tell, because nothing in my background had prepared me to be an expert in sherry. The end of my tutorial coincided with the serving of dinner in hall. I would have found it hard to imagine a more civilised way of life. I still hold that view.

Oxford, for me, was also a time to make lifelong friends. There was a tradition that on Mayday the choristers of Magdalene College gathered at dawn to sing ancient but joyful chants from the top of their college tower. The socially in thing was to listen to them from a punt floating on the river below. Punts, even though they are flat-bottomed and ungainly are – culturally speaking – the Oxford equivalent of Venetian gondolas. They are similar to gondolas only in the sense that they actually float, are steered and propelled thanks to a pole, and are one of the most effective ways of enticing girls into what, with a bit of luck, might turn out to be a romantic tryst – or at least that was the way it was in my day.

My friend Sean O'Connor and I had it all worked out. We would rent the punt the evening before, put wine and other appropriate provisions in it, moor it in a quiet spot upriver, pray for a rainless night so we could sleep on it for a few hours under blankets, pick up the girls who had agreed to join us and proceed to Magdalene Tower in the hope of weaving our way through the crush of competing punts. It was a good plan particularly since both Sean and I had high opinions of our punting skills.

I know not the name of the devil that made us do it but at some point in the early hours of the morning we were overtaken by wanderlust and committed the unforgivable sin of leaving our punt unattended. I would like to think that it was for no more than a few minutes but it could have been for a while longer; long enough, alas, that on our return the punt had disappeared – and not just the punt but the blankets, the chilled white wine and the fine biscuits we had planned to breakfast on so as to impress the girls. The girls? I don't even remember their names or from which college we were going to pick them up. We never did get to hear the choristers – we derisively referred to them as castrati – and the most humiliating part of the episode was the rebuke I received from my scout when the next day he attempted to make my blanket-less bed.

It was during the course of my second year at Oxford that I met Lisette Coghlan. There were relatively few Catholics at Oxford but we were a sociable lot, meeting for mass in a converted tunnel-shaped army hut made of corrugated iron. This was before Vatican II and English Catholics still had a strong sense of identity and an awareness that they belonged to a minority group that, since Elizabethan times, had been unfairly singled out for persecution. It was a curious feeling to be hearing mass in a disused army hut knowing we were surrounded by magnificent chapels and churches built prior the Reformation and rooted within the Catholic monastic tradition.

The chaplaincy was a good place to meet people and I for one enjoyed lingering for coffee after mass, or after meetings organised by an intellectually vibrant Newman Society. Lisette was in her first year. She sang in the chaplaincy choir and was a scientist studying zoology at Somerville, one of Oxford's four women's colleges. In those days the idea of admitting women to the other colleges would have been dismissed as dangerous and outlandish. As a consequence men hugely outnumbered women. I knew little about zoology but we had met over coffee and then later came across each other at a dance. Most colleges organised dances, generally in the summer, for the stated purpose of commemorating a historic event such as the college's foundation. Even though they were somewhat formal events, attendance was not limited to the members of that particular college; anyone willing to purchase a ticket was entitled to attend. I do not remember very much about who had invited whom but the fact is that we danced together and thereafter decided we wanted to see more of each other. It turned out that we both knew Sheila Cassidy, a medical student who was our senior both in years and in experience. She decided we were made for each and went out of her way to encourage our romance. Sheila would go on to achieve fame not only as a doctor dedicated to promoting hospice care in the UK but also as a writer whose first book, recounting her horrendous experience of arrest and torture in Chile under the Pinochet régime for having treated political dissidents, became a bestseller.

We might have been made for each other but that did not mean that things went smoothly. By the beginning of my third and last year at Oxford, we had given up seeing each other. While it was true that we had somewhat different backgrounds, those differences had little if anything to do with the break up. Lisette was an enthusiastic and lively person, we were attracted to each other and never had the slightest difficulty finding things to do together. The reasons were more complex. She had attended a convent school and felt drawn to the religious life. That was something I could relate to. I had also at one time given consideration to the priesthood. It was a way of life I knew myself to be, in many respects, well suited to. There is a contemplative streak to my character; I have an affinity for reflection and am drawn to the idea that compassion is something the world can profit from.

Lisette's decision initially caused me considerable emotional turmoil but my last year at Oxford turned out to be no less exciting and exhilarating than the others. I knew that this brush with paradise was coming to an end and I was determined to enjoy whatever remained of it to the utmost.

Then there was the awkward question of what I was going to do for a living. I knew full well that Oxford was not the real world – not by any stretch of the imagination – and that I would need money to live. This was the early 1960s and money was scarce. Teaching appealed to me – there was something of the scholar in me – but I also wanted to see the world. So what about journalism? Perhaps not a bad choice but I was too much of rebel to even consider following in my father's footsteps. How about something technical? I had always been interested in how things worked. As a child I pestered my grandmother with questions on every subject under the sun and when given the chance spent hours on end watching the local farmers go about their business, and not just the farmers, but also the workmen who tinkered with the old farmhouse. It was this curiosity for how things worked that had coloured my memories of the making of *The Fallen Idol*. If I liked puzzling out how things fit together maybe, someone suggested, I should try numbers. Not the numbers of mathematicians but the numbers people use to describe how things relate to each other.

That is how, barely a few days before taking the elaborate week-long exam that was designed to provide undergraduates with an opportunity to give some kind of account of what they might actually have studied over the previous three years, I put on my only suit and took the train to London. I was to be interviewed by Cooper Brothers, one of the venerable accounting firms in the City of London. In those days it would have occurred to no one to make out a curriculum vitae or anything like that – certainly not at Oxford, at any rate. The only thing the partner who talked to me cared about was who had recommended me – one of my father's distant banker cousins – and what school I had attended before university. To my relief, not a word was said about *The Fallen Idol*. He offered me the job on the spot. In total ignorance of what I had let myself in for, I accepted; also on the spot.

11

Exile In London

That September I took up my job at 33 Gutter Lane in the City of London: the most respectable of addresses. This was 1961 and in spite of the Cold War, in spite of Mao Tse-tung's China and in spite of France's increasingly futile attempt to make sense of the Algerian War the world felt like a predictable place. Its very predictability meant that I felt obliged to work in order to eat, pay rent and meet social expectations I was in no position to challenge. I didn't know it but it was a world that was about to change. I earned exactly £500 a year; exactly that is before all kinds of taxes. It was a pittance and not, it struck me, the kind of money people earn in the film business.

I was an articled clerk: a clerk in the mediaeval sense of belonging to a privileged class of people who had actually been taught to read and write, and articled because I was required to enter into a contract with a principal and subscribe my name to a list of articles, or contractual clauses. The principal was invariably a man – this was the 1960s – a partner in the firm, and therefore one of the holders of the coveted certification allowing him, and those working at his beck and call, to render professional services in exchange for fees.

Although the mediaeval aspects of the arrangement were beginning to give way to the realities of post-war Britain, we were still expected to act the part and put up with the quaintness of it all. One such requirement was that we wear dark suits, white shirts and bowler hats: a rolled up umbrella was not de rigueur but a sensible extra given London's high rainfall.

We neophyte articled clerks were introduced to the mysteries of accounting via an elaborate exercise involving a tea-importing merchant who for reasons that seemed to me wholly absurd insisted on recording each entry at least twice – actually often three times since we were expected to use journals and other books of prime entry out of deference to anachronistic practices that were reminiscent of Dickensian times. We were issued with red pens so we could make check marks in our clients' books, instructed in the precise way of penning these check marks, and given rubber stamps with the firm's initials [Inspected by CB&Co,] to prove we had actually looked at the invoices and other documents used by our clients.

That first year in London did feel like an exile from paradise but all was not lost. I found a room in a quiet street in Kensington with a family whose son I had known at Oxford and who was now at Yale and I even made do with my £500. My life had, however, changed in the most radical of ways.

Before reporting to work at Gutter Lane I visited my beloved grandmother in Normandy. She was increasingly frail and by now beset by chronic rheumatic pain. It was there that I received a letter from Lisette. I recognised her handwriting when I collected the post from our postbox at the top of the field. It took me by surprise: I had not imagined she would have reason to write to me.

We had seen very little of each other during that last year, so it was by chance that we came across each other at a party just a few days after I had finished taking my final exam. While I was leaving Oxford for good, she still had a year to go. I do not remember exactly what happened at this party or even where it was held, although I think it was some kind of picnic beside the river on a sunny afternoon, but the fact is that I had said something that she took to be directed at her and, on the spur of the moment, she came up and slapped me. What I remember more clearly is that we agreed to meet a couple of days later so as to put the matter behind us. It was a friendly meeting tinged for me with a feeling of regret that the attraction we had felt for each other in the past had not been allowed to take its course.

The letter changed all that. Was I willing to resume our relationship? Indeed, I was. After Lisette finished her last year at Oxford, she arranged to take a job in London with Macmillan's the publisher. As a junior editor of scientific books, she was not paid much more than I was, but she could afford to share a flat with two other girls just off Knightsbridge. From then on we saw plenty of each other. London's fabled theatre district offered lots of entertainment and seats up in the 'gods' were so cheap that even we could afford them. My employer provided me with Luncheon Vouchers, little blue tickets that were valued at three shillings and could be used in most restaurants, cafes, and pubs. Many were the evenings when Lisette and

I managed to eat something after a show and toss in a few blue tickets to help pay the bill.

By this stage in my life I had good reason to believe I had shaken off *The Fallen Idol* for good. I had at last achieved a state of happy anonymity. Not so fast! I have no idea how the BBC learned of my whereabouts but I was at work one morning checking a client's ledger: a damp, sooty outfit assembling gigantic printing machines imported from Germany in a warehouse next to Waterloo Station. 'You're wanted on the phone,' I was told. The caller asked me point blank whether I remembered Dora Bryan. I could have hung up but I didn't. I had fond memories of Dora. She had played the brief but engaging role of the young prostitute who had been asked by the police to wheedle information out of the frightened little boy. It was a key scene: the child was marooned in the police station after his night-time escape from what he imagined to be the scene of a heinous murder. Had I ever watched a TV show called *This is Your Life*? That was a tougher question to which the honest answer was hardly, if ever, but I did know it involved putting a famous person on stage and then inviting in, one by one, people that famous person had come across in the past. The idea was to surprise the famous person and then for everyone concerned to say clever and funny things. The show had been pioneered in America in the 1950s and then adapted for UK audiences where it met with enduring success. Unhesitatingly, I accepted. I liked the idea that Dora was to be the famous person. She had made a name for herself as Rita Tushingham's mother in a deservedly successful 1961 film *A Taste of Honey*. That was something Dora excelled at: a larger-than-life supporting role that added zest to the entire production.

Besides I was in need of stimulation: accounting, especially in its early stages, involves episodes of unremitting boredom. The clincher was that I was offered a £30 fee: hardly a fortune but in relationship to my annual salary of £500 not something to be passed up. I can't say I remember much about the actual show except that Dora was as gushing and welcoming as ever. She did, though, remember me as the little boy she had bounced on her knees on the police station set at Shepperton Studios. Dora and I were destined to meet again – many, many years later. Today I have all the more reason to be glad I had accepted the offer to appear on that silly TV show back in 1962.

The next morning my colleagues in the warehouse near Waterloo Station greeted me with puzzled looks. I had quite a bit of explaining to do and my cover, once again, was shot.

Articled clerks were expected to learn the academic aspects of their trade from a correspondence course that went by the Gilbert and Sullivanesque name of H. Foulkes Lynch. Weekly, we would post in completed tests for grading. All this sounds quite absurd to modern ears; given that we now live in an age of graduate business studies, of multiple degrees and of web-based learning techniques. But this archaic arrangement suited me well. I was studious and happy to be left alone to work at my own pace. Doing a postgraduate degree in philology would have been more fun, but deep down I found this to be an acceptable compromise. During that second year another good thing came my way.

One of the firm's most prestigious clients was Unilever, a business whose origins of which were traceable to the colonial expansion of the major European powers into Africa. Would I be willing to spend two months or so in the Congo? In June of 1960, Belgium, in the wake of the massive decolonisation movement of the late 1950s, had reluctantly granted independence to its vast Congolese possessions. Chaos had ensued, exacerbated by a civil war between the rich mineral province of Katanga to the south and the colonial capital of Léopoldville. Unilever had, against all odds, managed to hold on to some of its Congolese-based business. I would be paid a dangerous posting bonus and be given an extra £50 so I could purchase a tropical wardrobe. I imagined the pith helmets, khaki shorts and safari shirts of Hollywood films. This was a god-sent opportunity to toss aside my bowler hat for a while.

I flew into Brussels in late January 1963 with a colleague and spent a damp, foggy, wintry evening in the Grande Place drinking beer, listening to a couple of disgruntled Belgian corporate high-ups bemoaning the good old days and predicting that, for decades to come, the Congo would wallow in a post-colonial maelstrom of unremitting violence. The next evening I climbed into a Boeing 707 – these huge planes were one of the great innovations of the 1960s – for an eight-hour flight to Léopoldville. This was adventure. It occurred to me that if I had traded philology for this, then it was a fair trade and I should be willing to live by it. I did not feel shortchanged because on arrival in Leopoldville, I experienced for the first time in my life that out-of-the world feeling that comes from stepping into a vast sun-filled greenhouse full of beguiling earthy smells. It turned out to be another of my Proustian moments because whenever I smell that humid earthiness, I think back to that early morning in Léopoldville airport. After walking down a rusting ramp propped up against the silvery Boeing, we the passengers trudged along the tarmac until we reached a hut. There we were told to drop our passports into a large wooden box. It was the kind of box my grandmother might have used to store a small crop of turnips. Then we waited. It was a long wait but eventually a couple of Congolese soldiers dressed up as Belgian gendarmes came back into the hut with the turnip box. They emptied its contents on the floor and informed us in perfect French that if we wanted our passports back all we had to do was to get down on our knees and retrieve them. Welcome to the Congo, said the company chauffeur who had been waiting for us outside the hut.

The Unilever people whose books we had been sent to inspect treated us with a mix of wariness and deference. They wined and dined us hoping to tame our inquisitorial instincts with hard-luck tales of how their good work had been systematically undone by native incompetence. Fortunately, independence had not led to the collapse of all of Léopoldville's fine restaurants, so that I missed my three-shilling Luncheon Vouchers not one whit. They need not have worried because as auditors we were quite harmless. My only regret is that I had so few opportunities to travel outside the city. The dangers were real enough since armed bands roamed the countryside raping and pillaging. I did cross the Congo river – one of the world's great waterways – in an overcrowded ferry into Brazzaville, the capital of what had once been the French Congo where I watched kids play soccer in the streets and saw posters of the then president, a renegade priest who had a penchant for green cassocks. I felt privileged to have the chance to see such things. It was akin to an out-of-body experience: here I was peering in from above and watching myself walk and move in a world to which I did not really belong.

There's a sequence at the beginning of *The Fallen Idol* that takes place at London Zoo. To me there was something enchanting about it: a magic lantern world that is the background to a make-believe story and that somehow makes everything more real than reality itself. Likewise, peering into this African world to which I did not belong, brought about a sharpening of the senses – a glimpse of a reality that lies beyond the banality of day-to-day existence. Come to think of it, wasn't that what I had begun to discover within *The Fallen Idol* when decades later I began to see it through different eyes?

12

My Grandmother's Death

My parents had not yet retired and were still living in the same little Mayfair flat that had seen the family through the war years. I would, on occasion, drop by for dinner. My mother was not always around: she travelled to faraway places like Rome and Moscow on writing assignments for various magazines. And my grandmother, who was now in her mid 70s, was more and more dependent on my mother visiting her frequently.

I liked having dinner with my father. He was at the time fiction editor for the popular weekly magazine *Woman's Own.* He took pride in selecting well-written stories many of which were published weekly in serialised form. He paid particular attention to promising women writers and liked the job although, by his own admission, he felt ill suited to office politics: hence, I think, his increasing interest in retiring.

His office was on a busy street between Covent Garden and The Strand. He loved this part of London more than any other and always walked. He felt at home making his way through the vegetable barrows and stalls that had not yet been exiled from what he affectionately referred to as The Garden. J. M. Dent, the publishing firm known most particularly for its Everyman imprint, had for the longest time published the family's books. Dent's offices were at the edge of Covent Garden and on his way to Leicester Square my father invariably walked by the old-fashioned bow windows of their venerable wood panelled premises. Inside, the smell of freshly printed books mingled with wax. Rarely could my father resist walking in: it must have been immensely reassuring and grounding. Beyond Piccadilly Circus he would continue his walk through the maze of side streets until he reached Shepherd Market, but not without having picked up a packet or two of cod fillets and green peas from the freezer section of whatever grocer he happened to pass.

That was our meal, boiled unceremoniously in a saucepan atop the ancient gas stove that had stood there unadorned and immutable since the war years of my childhood. We ate, as we always had, around the kitchen table and on a newspaper. After the boiled cod and peas there was buttered bread and strawberry jam. I had grown to enjoy his conversation.

After the meal I would go back to my bed-sitter in Kensington. I had homework to do and he went right back to his typewriter. I admired his capacity for hard work.

Early one morning in 1962, my father telephoned with the news that my grandmother had died. He had already made arrangements to leave the following day for France so he could be with my mother. No, there was no reason for me to take time off work. He would prefer I not do so. It would be a simple funeral and there was no reason for me to come. Would I, however, come to dinner that evening? No, not at the flat, no deep frozen cod tonight, he wanted to eat at Wheeler's.

My parents were not people who ate in restaurants other than for professional reasons. Wheeler's, however, was special to them. It was in St. James's and next to the London Library, one of the magic places in my father's universe. Then right there, over the phone, my father startled me with a question. I had a girl friend, didn't I? Yes I did. My parents had never met Lisette. It should have come quite naturally for me to introduce her to my parents and yet I was wary. It was a wariness bred out of a realisation that whenever I had made my own decisions about things that really mattered to me it had generally led to some kind of conflict with my parents. I think my father sensed the nature of my wariness. It was almost as if there was an unspoken understanding between us: he would always side with my mother – he had to – but at the same time he also had a way of letting me know that it was up to me to make my own decisions and that he would respect me for that.

The three of us met that evening at Wheeler's. We ate oysters and fried sprats and my father ordered a bottle of Chablis. He was in an excellent mood, and Lisette remembers the meal to this day.

I thought a good deal about my grandmother. She had an enormous influence over me. She was my unfailing ally in a confusing and often anxiety-provoking world. She contributed immensely to the happiness of my childhood and had rooted me in the soil of that little piece of Norman countryside that became home to me like no other place on earth. She was also the first person through whom I witnessed the frightening intensity of physical pain.

She had suffered in other ways. Even as I child I had sensed the agony of the exile she had endured when the British troop ship carrying the remnants of her family had sailed out of Saint Malo in June 1940 leaving her alone and totally at the mercy of an immensely threatening world. The other thing I knew with blinding clarity about my beloved grandmother is that she had lost her son, my namesake Robert; Bébert as he was called, cherished and smothered with her kisses until that moment when, barely two years old, he was struck down by meningitis. I knew just enough about life to sense that this was an absurdity that defied human understanding. Even my mother, his elder sister, had kept his memory - and the pain that was inextricably interwoven with that memory - at the forefront of her own consciousness.

I should, of course, have joined my father the next day and made the Channel crossing so I could see my grandmother one last time before she was placed in her coffin.

I regret that decision to this day. My father had wanted to spare me the pain, but that was no excuse. I had, after all, already made plenty of important decisions for myself. I think, though, that death frightened me. Not so much the idea of dying - there was a religious streak in me that helped me deal with the inevitability of death - but its physical aspects, stiffness, decay and stench. I did not have the guts that evening to look beyond all that.

I knew my grandmother had died in her room - the one on the ground floor with the massive ancient stone walls that is beside the kitchen; the kitchen with its old Aga stove and the bumpy black and white checker-board floor tiles. I also knew that the local carpenter would make her coffin and that her body would have to be placed in it - right there in her room. It would then be propped up against two chairs until the arrival of the hearse the next day. That was why my father was about to take the night boat to Le Havre. He had told my mother he would be there to help lift up my grandmother's body into the box. He wanted to spare me that grim task. I should have been grateful to him, and in some ways I was, but death cannot just be held at bay. I had never seen, let alone touched, a dead body.

There were plenty of wakes in the Normandy village of my childhood but my parents had kept me away from them. Instead, I would watch the hearse go through the village on its way from the church to the cemetery that was beside the railway station and had been bombed by mistake by allied planes during the Battle of Normandy. I was terrified of the hearse – it was a frightening horse-drawn contraption that looked like a black-draped four-poster bed on large, gangly, spoked wheels. Black pompoms resembling fluffy mops surmounted each of the four posts. When the dead person was a child the pompoms were white, as was the horse. The horse was made to walk painfully slowly along the long avenue lined with coppiced plane trees that led to the station. That was so the procession of mourners could follow on foot. If it rained out came black umbrellas.

Yes, I regret I did not have the guts to attend my grandmother's funeral, or even see her one last time before she was placed in the box.

Much later I would remember that damp winter evening in Wheeler's, cosy and warm, eating the best oysters the world had to offer, and sipping Chablis. There I was sitting opposite my father and beside my future wife. I could not have possibly imagined that she and I would one day – in a mercifully distant future – endure our own loss and that it was a loss that would draw me ever closer to my beloved grandmother. By then death would have lost its fearful external trappings and would no longer be unfinished business. I would know it for what it really is: inexorable and to be faced up to in the light of love and of hope.

13

South America And Marriage

Why was it that when Lisette and I finally got married we decided to go and live in New York City? People do ask such questions – even people who have watched *The Fallen Idol* on the late night classic film reruns and are just plain curious. I have no coherent answer but it happened in a roundabout way.

The reason, I think, that I had put in all this blood and sweat over three long years to become an accountant is that I had this desire to see the world – not like a tourist – but involved in it and getting a big kick out of being there. So I told Lisette I wanted to go on just one more adventure before we got married – to South America. Lisette had always wanted to work as a researcher in a biological station so she would go to the Camargue in the South of France for six months.

I set my sights on Cali, a prosperous city in an Andean valley in one of Colombia's southern provinces. It was a matter of chance. I knew someone from school whose father was the local British consul and I thought a local address might come in useful. I took a room in a grubby little pension in Cali's colonial quarter beside a cavernous Franciscan church with an effusively baroque façade. Breakfast, lunch and dinner tasted much the same – generous servings of rice and beans. This was my first experience of Hispanic culture transposed to the Andes: a city laid out on a grid, snow-capped mountains in the far distance, open shop fronts, Indian women decked in colourful shawls hawking food in the streets and the Latin-accented rhythms of Africa blending with the plaintiveness of the Spanish soul. I felt quite at home.

The consul's wife invited me to parties at the local country club, where the moneyed white folk met. The men played cards, smoked oval shaped cigarettes packed with high performance tobacco, and drank locally distilled brandy from huge tulip shaped glasses. The women chatted interminably about children and grandchildren and complained about their servants. The young – creatures of the 60s – swung on the dance floor under the watchful eyes of their scheming mothers. I plotted my escape.

It was a job. Price Waterhouse, the granddaddy of the accounting profession, had an office in town. I was offered a salary that seemed generous – enough to pay for my daily rice and beans several times over. The man in charge was a Scot, a sly fox, my Colombian co-workers informed me on my first day in the office. Within days I was on a plane with a colleague to Quito, the capital of Ecuador – a charmingly preserved colonial city set high up in the Andes, and surrounded by Indians in traditional dress. The hotel had stunning views of the snow-capped Western Andes. It was in Quito that I first experienced the breathlessness of high places and understood the profound impact of altitude on everything from vegetation to culture.

We went from client to client auditing their books as best we could: we were strictly on our own, the phone system was inoperable and there were no faxes, no Internet, and no computers of any kind. Every few weeks we flew back to Cali with briefcases stuffed with work papers. The supreme arbiter of the adequacy of our work was a large intimidating man in his late 30s who went by the name of Morgan. Morgan sat in shirtsleeves behind a large desk in the Cali office. He struck me, because of his short-cropped blond hair, clean-shaven appearance and intense seriousness, as the quintessential Yank – an image I must have formed exclusively from watching films. He made a big deal of telling me he was from Newark, New Jersey, and that I, ignorant barbarian that I was, was not to confuse his birthplace with the City of New York. Perish the thought!

During the latter part of the 16th century one of Queen Elizabeth I's privateers – another Morgan – had famously harassed the Spanish settlements on the Caribbean coast in search of loot and treasure. Legend has it that generations of Colombian mothers have kept their offspring in line by threatening them with the mere mention of the man's name; ruthless heretic that he undoubtedly was! We, the worker bees confined to the staff room in the back of the office, unhesitatingly referred to the man from Newark as *El Pirata*.

There was more to Ecuador than charming colonial Andean cities. Although a small country, it was a major banana producer. The bananas grew in huge plantations along the low-lying Pacific coast. One of our clients manufactured the cardboard boxes used for packing hands of green bananas for shipment to the United States. Boxes were trucked to the many packing stations that dotted the lowlands. El Pirata sent me on the most improbable of errands – I was to carry out a physical count of banana boxes so we could judge the reasonableness of the inventory carried on the box manufacturer's balance sheet.

On a map I circled the names of five plantations and asked to be taken to them. Map in hand, I hitched rides in company trucks going along dirt roads from village to village. The villages were no more than strips of corrugated iron-roofed huts, each with its complement of bars, tyre-repair shops, general stores and family-owned restaurants with tables set beside charcoal-burning stoves and crates of cola bottles. Pigs, chickens, sad and hungry-looking dogs and countless young children wandered aimlessly in and out of the clutter – especially when the harshness of the tropical sun had given way to the cooler stillness of the evening hours. I remember the uncompromising brightness of the kerosene lamps, the ubiquitous music – joyous, rhythmic, sounds of faraway Africa mingling with Spanish ballads and the wistfulness of Indian melodies – long lines of empty beer bottles and hammocks hooked up to ceiling beams.

As for banana trees they were everywhere. We drove hour after hour seeing nothing but their giant, shiny, arched leaves, and among them occasional groups of machete-wielding men, sombre in their tattered clothes and rubber sandals. This was a great expanse of green, a desert of sorts, a vast blanket of humid sameness with the power to burden the souls of those trapped within it. Much later, when I read Gabriel García Márquez's masterpiece *A Hundred Years of Solitude*, I realised that this was the world he had known as a child and that he had made into the backdrop of a melancholy landscape from which only those endowed with the gift of fantasy could escape. He thoroughly deserved his Nobel Prize.

At the end of my six-month stint the Scotsman-in-charge and El Pirata from Newark asked me to stay on. I was, they argued, ideally suited to making the best of tropical Cali's creature comforts. 'If ever you tried to make a living in New York, you'd be eaten alive,' El Pirata assured me in a good cop, semi-confidential 'I'm your friend after all' voice. I was flattered by the blandishments but miffed and challenged by the put down. It was then that I decided that the obvious thing was to try my luck in New York. Besides, Colombian society was becoming increasingly violent: politically motivated murders were commonplace, as were highly publicised kidnappings, especially of the wealthy that were routinely held up to ransom. These were ominous signs, even though I was far from suspecting that Colombia was on the brink of becoming one of the key players in the emerging global cocaine business.

The boys in the backroom gave me a grand old going away party that ended up in a brothel in the early hours of the morning – a friendly establishment where it was perfectly acceptable just to sit around in good company speculating on the meaning of life and downing countless inkpot-sized glasses of moonshine. I took it as a formative cultural experience that served me in good stead when years later I began to read in earnest the great Latin American novelists of the time, among them Mario Vargas Llosa – another future Nobel laureate – who was a great connoisseur of such establishments.

It was when I found myself on a flight bound for New York City that it came to me that a new phase of my life was about to begin. El Pirata's warnings about the perils of New York and the realisation of just how few dollars were left over from my Colombian savings caused me to experience a mild bout of anxiety. I need not have worried; subway tokens cost 15 cents a piece, as did a cup of coffee and, thanks to a friend, I found a room at the YMCA on Lexington Avenue. My interview with the venerable firm of Lybrand Ross Bros and Montgomery on lower Broadway turned out to be disappointingly uninspiring. The personnel manager glanced at my handwritten résumé and our conversation ran along the lines that if I wanted a job, well of course I could have one. As we parted he presented me with the firm's commentaries on the federal tax system: a hardbound 1,500-page tome, weighing several pounds. 'Welcome to the United States,' the man in a red tie, white shirt and polyester suit said to me, 'you can always dip into this during your honeymoon. It's a good introduction to what we stand for.' I was hired!

It was April of 1965, Lyndon Johnson was president, and the Vietnam War was about to erupt with cataclysmal force on the American psyche. I left New York bound for Paris.

Lisette came up from the Camargue and we met at Orly airport. Things did not go as planned: she was having second thoughts about marriage, about losing her independence. I have no clear recollection of what I said in reply. I do remember, though, deciding in my own mind that I still wanted to get married – that I was the marrying kind.

The idea of making a fresh start in New York must have also played into my own hankering for independence: from the complexity of my past: from my relationship with my parents and from my ambivalent feelings about *The Fallen Idol*.

The part about going to New York did not seem to bother Lisette in the least. She had her own way of dealing with adventure and accepted that it was an important - perhaps even a vital - part of her own life. I do not recall how long our conversation at Orly airport lasted but what I do, of course, remember is that by the time we got on the bus going into Paris our marriage was back on track.

There was nothing to be gained by waiting. The job in New York required a work visa. Since Lisette was born in the United Kingdom she could, under a highly favourable quota system, obtain a coveted green card giving permission to work within just a few weeks of applying for one at a US Embassy. Since I was French born, my own application would have entailed a much longer wait. It was suggested we solve the problem by marrying and then making a joint application. Ours was therefore a hasty but gracious wedding held in a church in Kemerton a few miles from Bredon, the Worcestershire village where Lisette's parents lived. The Oxford University Catholic chaplain, a kindly and spiritual priest to whom we had both grown attached, married us. Lisette's uncle gave an afternoon tea party after which Lisette and I left for our honeymoon. We drove away with only a vague idea about where we would spend it. True to form, I had made no hotel reservations - not for our first night together and nor for any other.

My parents maintained their opposition to our marriage. It was not a strong opposition - more of a wish that somehow the whole unwelcome intrusion into their lives would just go away. My father's lame excuse for not attending our wedding was that he and my mother had just retired to Normandy and that returning to England might jeopardise their tax status. Lisette's parents must have thought their daughter was marrying into a particularly odd family. Blanche, the younger of my two spinster aunts, was the only member of my family present. I, of course, quite inured to such strangeness, thought little of it.

14

Children

The first of our two children, our daughter Dominique, was born in Manhattan on a snowy January day in 1970. Lisette and I were in our fifth year of living in New York. We had arrived in New York under very different circumstances: on one of those warm steamy days that are so typical of August in the city. We were equally excited but, obviously, for very different reasons. Back then, we were still on our honeymoon and had crossed the Atlantic on the *Queen Mary* - that grand old lady that was on the cusp of retirement. We had packed the little we possessed in a couple of small trunks and our biggest concern was finding an apartment. Denis Woodfield, the only American we knew - we had met him at Oxford - helped us find one. There was nothing to it and in no time at all we were settled in an Upper East Side studio apartment for $160 a month. I had a job - with the people on Lower Broadway who thought I should read their tax book on my honeymoon - and it took Lisette no more than a couple of weeks to find hers with a publisher, as an editor of science text books.

We had made a grand time of it. At the end of our first year we had driven to San Francisco and back in a VW bus. After four years on the East Side we were now living in a larger apartment in Greenwich Village. We had come to New York with the intention of spending a year, or perhaps two, and then returning to Europe. That thought was long gone.

I had changed my job and was now working with a bank. I had been lucky with jobs and there was really nothing wrong with the one I had left. It might even be that it would have been better had I stayed put. It is one thing to be lucky with jobs but quite another to fit comfortably within the expectations inherent in actually doing one. For me a job was a compromise with the dulling harshness of what it took to earn a living. There was an idealistic streak in me that pushed back - sometimes hard - against the conditions that were part of that bargained-for compromise. I came to call

121

it the *Paradise Lost* feeling. The fact is that my first job had come to me at an unusually early age. What did it feel like to actually film *The Fallen Idol*, to be in it, I am sometimes asked. Well, it was a job. You were told where and when to show up, you did what you were asked to do and by the end of the day there was this nice feeling that you had earned the right to go home. It was a compromise. I would probably have preferred to be in Normandy with my grandmother and the chickens or reading a good book, or dreaming away: they described me back then as a fidgety dreamer! But there was something engaging – stimulating, actually – about having to deal with other people – difficult, but engaging – and the doing part was exciting: especially if the doing involved seeing and experiencing new things. So the fact was that New York was a pretty fair compromise.

Lisette and I sat in a cab racing up Sixth Avenue to the Roosevelt Hospital on the Upper West Side: her contractions had begun in the early hours of the morning. That was an event that really did change our lives. We named our daughter Dominique not after anyone in either of our families but simply because there was something harmoniously pleasing about the name. She was a healthy, normal baby and the news of her birth gave much pleasure to both Lisette's and my parents – she was their first grandchild.

Our move to Greenwich Village in the summer of 1969 happened to coincide with a far greater awareness on our part of just how deep and passionate opposition to the Vietnam War had become: especially among those younger than we. It was then that I realised that even though we were only just 30, Lisette and I belonged, like it or not, in the ranks of an older generation that had experienced school in the old fashioned way – largely without drugs and without the free-for-all that was to characterise the landmark events of what came to be known as the Hippie Generation. Not that we did not witness first hand the student demonstrations triggered by the Tet Offensive in 1968, nor did we hesitate to wheel Dominique's pram – decorated with numerous Peace buttons – among the pot-smoking love-in groups that thronged Washington Square in 1970, but we were in a sense already outsiders peering in at a perplexingly changing world that was not of our making.

Dominique seemed to catch more than her fair share of colds and at times slept fitfully through coughing and wheezing. On one occasion in particular we stayed up with her trying to understand why she cried so insistently and for no apparent reason. I was totally perplexed not knowing whether to ascribe her behaviour to a succession of wilful temper tantrums, or to some unfathomable illness. Finally, exhausted, we took her to the emergency department at nearby St. Vincent's Hospital. She was sedated and put under an oxygen tent: only later, and amid confusing and conflicting diagnostics, did it transpire that she was asthmatic, and not only asthmatic but also subject to allergies. Lisette had noticed that her lips had become swollen on contact with a spoonful of peanut butter.

Lisette and I were deeply upset by Dominique's stay at St. Vincent's; perhaps I even more than Lisette since I had totally misjudged the situation, blaming it on a bad case of tantrums; something, as I saw it at the time, stern discipline could surely overcome. I had shown myself to be impatient and irrational in my scolding of my baby daughter. I was very new at being a parent. In the light of subsequent events that would make me painfully aware of the full implication of what had happened that night, I now wished I had been far more humble and sensitive to the need to empathise and listen to my daughter's needs. That incident remains one of my great regrets. The events of that night should also have taught me something about my relationship with my own parents: have made me more indulgent of their own failures in dealing with me.

Our son, Edward, was born under very different circumstances. Dominique was into her third year - growing up happily and normally - when Lisette became pregnant a second time. Then something happened to once again bring about a sudden change in our lives. I had developed a close working relationship with a colleague at the bank who, much to my chagrin, had left to take up a job with a small investment bank headquartered in Tokyo.

One evening at home, after work, I received an unexpected call from Tokyo. It was Peter Wodtke, my former work colleague. Would Lisette and I be interested in joining him in Singapore? It was a job offer. Peter was in the process of moving the headquarters of the investment company, of which he was now president, to Singapore - a less expensive city than Tokyo and nearer to the South Eastern Asian countries which were the focus of the bank's investment activities. Would I be willing to fly to Tokyo for an interview over a long weekend? There was enthusiasm in Peter's voice. From the moment I had begun working with him, he had told me how the years he had spent with Citibank in Hong Kong had caused him to fall head-over-heels in love with Asia.

Lisette and I hardly hesitated. We relished the excitement of living in a part of the world that was totally foreign to us and we still felt young enough to face the challenge of bringing up young children in an unfamiliar environment. Leaving my present employer, however, turned out to be no fun and there were ruffled feathers aplenty. I still had much to learn when it came to smoothing over business relationships. On our way to Asia we stopped off in Europe: first we visited my parents in Normandy and then, after I had left for Singapore, Lisette went on to spend a few weeks in England with her mother who was now a widow. To Lisette's great sorrow, her father had died three years earlier of a massive and totally unexpected heart attack. His death, by a curious coincidence, had occurred on the occasion of Lisette's first visit to her parents after Dominique's birth.

It was spring in Normandy, a delightful time full of freshness and promise: the apple trees were flowering, as were the primroses in the hedgerows around the ancient house. One afternoon, my father took me aside and expressed surprise that Lisette was expecting a second child. 'Isn't life simpler with just one?' he asked wistfully. I knew that both my parents had views about the wisdom of having but one child. Views influenced, perhaps, by medical advice given to my mother about the danger to her of bearing another child. I had the wisdom to say nothing. Later, I was grateful that my father had not lived long enough to realise the foolishness of what he had said. He was, after all, just a fallible human being: a realisation that, as I grew older and wiser, actually drew me closer to him.

Edward was born that November, 1973, in a small hospital in one of Singapore's leafy and cosy neighbourhoods. I was present in the squeaky-clean delivery room. The attending doctor wanted to know what I thought about the stock market – right there in the delivery room. It was very Chinese and in sharp contrast to that January morning some four years earlier when Dominique was born. The delivery room at the Roosevelt Hospital in Manhattan was clean and efficient but it had none of the aggressive spotlessness of the Singapore clinic.

We had the good fortune to rent from the Singapore government one of the houses it had inherited from the British. Built in the 1930s to accommodate one of the many senior officials administering colonial Malaya, it was spacious, airy and charming with a red tile roof and a sweeping view over the distant Straits – the strategic navigable body of water separating the Malay Peninsula from Indonesia. It had a hilltop garden with flowering hibiscus hedges, bougainvillaea, coconut and mango trees and papaya bushes. Below was a Malay village with a small mosque and a large brick building that, so the story went, had before the war served as a government-operated opium factory. Unlike most expatriates who fancied chauffeured cars, I was quite content to walk down each morning to the main road below and catch a bus for a ten-minute ride to the business district. The house came with a gardener, a male cook and a housemaid. The machete-wielding gardener was a large man, a Tamil Indian with a smile that was both constant and toothless and a richly dark shiny complexion, who day-in-day-out went about his gardening clad in a mere loincloth. He had a knack for climbing the trunks of coconut trees, barefoot and seemingly effortlessly.

The company I had come to Singapore to work for, PICA, was a strange bird. Each of its 200 or so shareholders – they were among the world's largest companies – had pitched in a bit of money so they could claim to be doing something good for the struggling third world. Our directors – senior executives drawn from our prestigious roster of Japanese, American and European shareholders – expected us to invest wisely, profitably and safely but also in accord with the lofty ideal of nurturing local needy capitalists. 'Do good,' might have been the motto held out to us, 'but don't embarrass us by losing so much as a penny of our money.' They also expected to be treated with great deference and were above all interested in hobnobbing with each other. It seemed at times as if my friend Peter and I were running a mini United Nations for their exclusive benefit.

The irony is that the two countries that were, in time, to drive the formidable engine of Asian economic success were closed to us. China was impenetrable; it was in the throes of one of the most convulsive events in its history – the Cultural Revolution, ruthless and irrational, run amok. India was likewise a no-man's-land: not because of political upheaval, but because business was deliberately hobbled by a Kafkaesque attachment to red tape. That left us with the Southeast Asian nations (Indonesia, Malaysia, the Philippines, Singapore and Thailand) plus Taiwan, South Korea and Hong Kong. While full of opportunities each of these countries presented us with particular challenges. Singapore was too rich and successful to be in need of development capital while neighbouring Malaysia, a beautiful, orderly country on the surface, was in fact devilishly complex politically. The local Chinese business owners had no need to be given lessons in capitalism, since they were thriving on their own family-based version. What they needed, though, was to find ways of coexisting with their politically dominant Muslim Malay neighbours whom they secretly despised for their lack of enthusiasm for business. Much the same could be said for Thailand where a significant part of the financial and business community was in the hands of a seemingly integrated Chinese minority who knew a thing or two about currying favour with the Thai political elite. Then there was Indonesia – the OK Corral of investing where foreigners like us had to pretend we had never heard of bribery and where the juiciest goodies were reserved for the numerous army generals who camped out at the state-run oil monopoly. Not to forget the Philippines – charming, welcoming and in need of our money but smothered by President Marcos and his equally dictatorial wife (the infamous Imelda with her closet full of shoes) and struggling with an inefficient agrarian economy unable to support its growing population. There was also Taiwan, a thriving beehive of activity, but overwhelmingly dominated by family-run business clans whose patriarchs had accompanied Chiang Kai-shek in 1949 as he fled from the mainland pushed out by Mao's People's Army. Finally, South Korea was a hectic place doing its best to imitate the Japanese economic miracle and where we foreigners were tolerated but made to feel we did not really belong.

This was 1973, the year of the famous Oil Crisis: the Arab oil producers had, following the Yom Kippur war, pledged to halt oil exports to Israel's supporters, and OPEC decreed an astronomical increase in the price of crude oil. Richard Nixon was still president – the Watergate affair was in full swing and would lead to his resignation in August of the following year. Western nations were in virtual economic recession and the values of currencies – the dollar in particular – were being undermined by ubiquitous inflation. It was nonetheless the most interesting of times and, for Lisette and for me, Singapore was a remarkably comfortable place to live in and from which to travel.

Our children shared our good fortune and thrived. Dominique, however, had not outgrown her asthma attacks. Why did she seem healthier while on vacation – in Normandy in particular? Was it due to there being less pollution? But then there were cats and pollen aplenty in Normandy. Could, Lisette wondered, the daily stress of attending school be a contributing factor? She was certainly unusually susceptible to virus infections. So were her frequent colds to blame for the severity of her attacks?

As we were about to leave Normandy to begin our fourth year in Singapore, my parents asked Lisette permission to keep Dominique, then six, with them till the end of the summer? It seemed like a good idea. September came and went. Dominique was in good health, we were told, and was on the verge of speaking decent French. She was happy writing and reading. Did we realise, my parents asked, how bright she was? So yes, in the end Dominique stayed with them for the best part of a year. The ancient house once inhabited by my grandmother was still working its magic.

Lisette and I faced a stark choice: either live out our lives as expatriates in Asia or come home. Surprisingly, perhaps, home was now the United States. We had not abandoned our European roots – far from it – but home was where we had first lived as a married couple. There is nothing simple about identity!

I had, meanwhile, come to realise that I was better suited to consulting and problem solving than to banking. I contacted my old firm, Lybrand Ross Bros and Montgomery, that had moved from Lower Broadway to Midtown Manhattan. My old boss readily agreed to my returning as a partner: would I, however, be willing to spend a few years in the Washington D.C. office before coming back to New York? Why ever not? I would, within a couple of years, be turning 40 and I sensed my job-hopping days had come to an end.

Lisette and I found a cosy little brick house in Bethesda beside a park. It was 1977, Jimmy Carter was president, the country was in an economic slump, the Japanese were thought to be about to take over the world, China was recovering from the Cultural Revolution, and everyone worried about inflation and energy costs. We, however, marvelled at how relaxed everyone was in the nation's capital: there were magnolias, cherry blossoms in spring, walks along the Potomac and concerts at the Kennedy Centre.

Our children attended a nearby school where most subjects were taught in French. Dominique made the best if it. She loved reading, had a highly developed imagination and a passion for writing. Her spelling was atrocious and she rebelled when it came to learning facts by rote. Edward was four years younger and it began to dawn on us how different he was. He lived in a world where spatial relationships were all important and within which he delighted in creating images in exquisite detail. The workings of his mind led him to places that were beyond the ken of others and made him ill suited not so much to institutional learning, but to the pace at which schools expect students to progress. Before long he was experimenting with depth, shading and contrast and his pictures were taking on symbolic qualities. There was nothing easy about any of this: not for us parents and certainly not for our children.

In Washington, Dominique's health improved, or so it seemed. The asthma, though, was still present, as were the inhalers she took everywhere with her, and the allergies. Once at a neighbourhood birthday party she choked on a brownie, badly, although she recovered quickly. We, of course, were learning about peanuts, as was she.

After our two years in Washington we made the move back to New York so I could take charge of the firm's international tax consulting practice. It was a job I was emotionally and intellectually suited to – probably the best compromise I could have come up with given my enduring struggle with those *Paradise Lost* feelings – and it would tide me over into retirement, almost 20 years later. Lisette and I reasoned that it would be better for our young children, and for Dominique's asthma in particular, that we live outside the City. So it was that we bought a 50-year-old New England clapboard saltbox with dormer windows. It was in Greenwich, Connecticut, and I resigned myself to being a daily commuter. Another compromise! The nicest thing about it was the wooded hillock beside the house, the stream that ran through it, the charm of the rocky outcrops and the numerous oaks and maples screening off the neighbours' houses: all on one acre tucked away from the road and just under two miles from the railway station – close enough for a daily walk – and a primary school no more than a mile away. The sellers had assured us that we were buying a happy house – no ghosts!

The consulting business was booming and globalisation – we called it by other names – was irresistibly fashionable. We were lucky to be caught up in such prosperity and, so far as we could tell, it would just go on and on. Lisette was equally busy: with our growing children, of course, but also as a science writer with an interest in education and then, in partnership with three other women, running a video business with ties to the community. Later, she joined the science staff of the local museum.

Our two children coped well enough with their schooling, especially Dominique who made the most of the four years she spent at the local high school. She developed a number of close friendships, wrote engagingly on social issues – several of her articles were published in local newspapers – and, thanks to her natural curiosity and enthusiasm, prospered academically. Her asthma had not gone away – Lisette and I knew by now that it would not. The steroid drugs she took to control it and to minimise her other respiratory difficulties brought about hard-to-cope-with debilitating side effects. Over and over again we wished it had been otherwise.

She and her brother were close. For Edward there could be no greater pleasure than to have a warm-hearted elder sister to humour him along. He gravitated towards a private school just a few minutes walk from our house. There he found teachers willing to tolerate his idiosyncratic learning habits and nurture his artistic abilities. He was lucky because it became apparent that, given time and encouragement, he also was capable of achieving excellence.

Each year our two children spent part of the summer in Normandy and in Worcestershire, with their respective grandmothers, who were both widows - my father had died of a sudden heart attack in his 81st year - and both welcoming of their visits. For Dominique and Edward these were indeed formative years.

While all this was going on I took a far-reaching decision to pursue something rather unusual. Why did I, a busy professional with a family, take on such a time consuming commitment? Precisely, I think, because I wanted to set aside a part of my life - even if it was a relatively small part of it - with which to do something radically different. I had colleagues who seemed unwilling, or maybe just unable, to place limits over the time and energy they dedicated to pursuing their professional careers. That frightened me, and it was something I talked to Lisette about. It scared me, I think, because I had been brought up with the idea that there was a side to each of us that was spiritual and needed nurturing. It was also very much part of my old struggle with those recurring feelings of *Paradise Lost* - a label I had given to feelings that defied description!

So why not become a deacon, a friend suggested? That was a bit of a mystery: a new thing as far as married men were concerned and thought up during Vatican II: an opportunity to do things like preach and visit the sick. It involved, I was told, several years of part time study: scripture, theology and the like. You would like the study part, my friend said, and they will want you to involve your wife so talk to Lisette about it. I did and then I spoke to the priest of the parish we had just joined who hardly knew me but encouraged me to apply.

There were tests and a session with a psychologist. I had never knowingly spoken to one before. Maybe I should have. There were things about my life that had not come easily: being an only child, compromising with the business of earning a living and then - were I to be brutally honest about it - occasionally experiencing moments of depression. These were times when whatever conflict I was wrestling with had dragged me down into a dark place of mental unresponsiveness from which there was no immediate escape. The part that concerned me was that it was my wife who bore the brunt of these incidents. As long as the feeling dissipates within a few hours, the man said me, use it as a way of empathising with the pain of others.

He suggested, though, that I might have reached the stage in my life when such things deserve reflection: as a way of coping with the difficulties that inevitably come our way. Looking back, as it were, with grown-up eyes – not his words, but mine.

I failed to tell him that I had been a child star and experienced the headiness of fame – a potent drug – and then the whipsawing pain that came from being treated as an ugly duckling in the schoolyard. I made no mention of it because *The Fallen Idol* had receded into the background: during the years spent in Asia, most especially. I had no desire to revisit it.

They accepted me. It took three years: a study weekend once a month away from home, weekly meetings, plenty of homework and, finally, in June of 1984, I was ordained with four other men. Ronald Reagan, that erstwhile film star who was present at the Royal Command Performance in London in 1948 where it had fallen to me to present a bouquet to the Queen, was President and the world seemed to be on the mend.

Had I during that considerable span of years – from Lisette and I arriving in New York as newlyweds to my finally coming to terms with the need to welcome stability into my life – finally shaken loose of my acting past? Had *The Fallen Idol*, and everything connected with it, at last *really* gone away?

The truth is that it had not: people just knew about my past. They were nice about it but I had that sneaking feeling that somehow it came up when people referred to me – particularly when I was out of earshot. "By the way... it's a funny thing... and you'd never guess... but..."

I remember one incident in particular. My office was mid-town in a handsome building on the west side of Sixth Avenue adjacent to the Rockefeller Centre. It came up that *The Fallen Idol* was playing at the Thalia cinema. I had no idea it was, but someone had taken notice.

Lisette and I had discovered the Thalia soon after coming to New York in the mid-1960s. It was on the upper reaches of Broadway, just north of 95th Street and the place in the city to see classic films – admission ran to no more than a few dollars and there were often double billings. The Thalia had been around since the early 30s and had acquired something of a cult status: it was even featured in Woody Allen's *Annie Hall* – itself a cult film for those who wanted to believe that Manhattan was the centre of the universe. This was the early 1980s and the Thalia was still operating.

A couple of my colleagues decided that our entire department – secretaries and all – should troop up to the Thalia to see the film: even Lisette was asked to show up with Edward and Dominique. It was a bright summer evening and we trekked over en masse to the Broadway line subway station on 51st Street. I decided to treat the whole crazy business as something of a joke and just put up with it. I had not seen the film for years and I did not even remember ever having seen it with Lisette, certainly not with our children. Dominique and Edward were both bemused, I think, to be peering into something that had happened long ago and that seemed to have no connection whatever with the person they understood their father to be. Lisette was just amused by the whole thing – aware of the fact that I had developed complex allergies triggered by the mere mention of *The Fallen Idol* and that it was time I grew up and put up with it. It felt decidedly odd – not unpleasantly so, but it did strike me that this was an awkward juxtaposition of two hitherto quite separate worlds. Edward was nine at the time and everyone that evening kept saying he now looked just like I had looked in the film. It is a fact that as a nine-year-old Edward did have blonde hair and an impish way about him.

Then something else happened: something decidedly strange. It was in the summer of 1988 – I could not forget the date. I received a phone call from a man called Ray Cabana who lived at other end of Connecticut close to the Massachusetts border. He introduced himself as a film buff and made much of the fact he had tracked down my mother's whereabouts in France, written to her asking how he might contact me and that she had scribbled my telephone number on a scrap of paper and returned it to him in a pre-addressed envelope. He could not believe it was a Connecticut number. Yes, he really, really wanted to meet me. Impressed by such tenacity, Lisette and I invited him to spend a Saturday afternoon with us. He came down with a friend and, to my great surprise, brought with him a 16-millimeter black-and-white copy of *The Wonder Kid* – spooled and stored in a couple of old-fashioned flat circular tin cans – together with a projector.

I have no idea how he had obtained a copy of the film. He struck me though as a film buff extraordinaire, a real bloodhound who, notwithstanding his apparent shyness and mild manners, would stop at nothing to track down a quarry. He was proud to have co-authored a highly professional looking and enthusiastic book on Peter Lorre, an Austrian born actor who had made a name for himself in Hollywood and had, among his credits, a supporting role in *Casablanca.*

After lunch, we set the projector up in our darkened basement and all of us watched *The Wonder Kid.* Our two children were with us. Dominique had just graduated from high school and was getting ready to begin her first year at university in Manhattan. She sat at the back watching, quite bemused by the whole business.

I was pleasantly surprised: wonderful scenery, good photography, decent acting – remember Oskar Werner – and pleasing overall. Not produced by Carol Reed! Of course not, nor was the flimsy storyline comparable in any way to what Graham Greene might have been inspired to write! There are things that are simply not repeatable. It, was, however, good enough.

Our visitors were quite charming. Ray Cabana was elated and, before leaving, mentioned he was going to write up the visit and have an article published in a local paper in his part of Connecticut. He had taken pictures of us all for that very purpose.

Then we forgot about Ray Cabana and about his promise of an article. He had visited us in the summer of 1988 and Lisette and I, unsuspecting, were about to live through the watershed event that would forever change our lives. The following March a copy of a newspaper article did come in the mail. It included pictures, some archival from *The Fallen Idol* and others taken by Ray during his visit, of our family including, of course, our daughter Dominique. Ray had no idea of what had befallen us and, in the article, spoke of Lisette and of me having a beautiful family. They are, he is quoted as saying at the end of the article, 'so nice that you feel that the outside world could hurt them'.

I can but wonder what had inspired Ray to utter such haunting words.

I am deeply grateful, though, to Ray for his visit. It is thanks to him that we all watched *The Wonder Kid* in our basement. I cannot, however, think of his visit or even reread these words, or even think of *The Wonder Kid* without experiencing a painful tightening of my throat and an equally painful swelling at the back of my eyelids. Such things come, I suppose, with looking back on life through grown-up eyes.

15

The Watershed

In 1988 Lisette and I had been married over 20 years, and nine had gone by since we had moved into our little white clapboard Connecticut house. That autumn Lisette and I, accompanied by Edward, had the thrill of driving Dominique into Manhattan on a bright sunny afternoon so she could start her new life as a student at Columbia University. She had turned 18 the previous January and was immensely proud to have been accepted at Barnard College. She had set her mind on becoming a professional writer and it was obvious to anyone who knew her that she was well on her way to achieving that ambition.

Dominique came home at the end of her first term. She, Edward – who missed his big sister – Lisette and I had planned to fly to Guatemala for a 10-day break from work and school. We left on Christmas day. Lisette and I, as must by now be obvious, love travelling and I have a particular affinity for Latin America. Since Dominique was born in Manhattan in early January 1970, her 19th birthday was just a few weeks away.

We had driven from Guatemala City into the western highlands, through stretches of unspoiled cloud forest and stayed two nights beside a stunningly beautiful lake surrounded by a ring of extinct volcanoes. We arrived in Chichicastenango on the morning of December 29, 1988 under a bright morning sky and it happened to be market day. This is an ancient city that has preserved its colonial heritage. The central square is vast, bound at each end by a church: one larger than the other but both are twin-towered and have whitewashed façades that sparkle in the tropical sun. A succession of adobe shops and dwellings with awnings and tiled roofs run lengthways along each side. The large size of the square is testimony to the fact that Indians have been gathering in Chichicastenango for centuries: well before the Spaniards came to this proud and beguiling land. They have been coming to this very place to sell their brightly coloured woven shawls, clay pots, beaded jewellery, corn, and vegetables. All day we feasted our eyes.

We planned to spend just one night in Chichicastenango and then drive back to Guatemala City to take a short flight to Tikal, one of the finest Mayan archaeological sites in Central America. This was a much-anticipated treat that was to be the last stage of our vacation. Our hotel in Chichicastenango was a splendidly appointed colonial era house: two-storied, built of wood and adobe with a central patio hung with orchids and poinsettias. From our rooms, the four of us watched dusk, and then night settle over the little town that by now felt quiet and almost deserted. Smoke rose from the nearby hills and families gathered around their evening meal.

We had eaten a good lunch and decided on a simple place where we could order a light meal. That was something I had suggested. We could have eaten in the hotel where there was a fancy, costlier restaurant. The four of us walked along the empty square and passed the floodlit whitewashed façade of the church we had visited earlier in the day. A group of solemn-faced, hatted, older men in dark jackets were swinging censers – simple censers made of tin cans – letting off clouds of sweet smelling incense. From the street the incense swingers looked like shadow puppets on a raised stage silhouetted against a screen: a ritual worship to gods who had dwelt in these mountains long before the arrival of the Spaniards.

I do not remember what the four of us ordered – omelettes perhaps – but towards the end of the meal Dominique ordered a hot chocolate drink. The evening had turned cooler and she was wearing a sweater. She took a few sips of the hot drink and almost immediately sensed something was wrong. It was a tightening feeling within her lungs. She had fortunately brought in her handbag an emergency dose of epinephrine (adrenalin) in an injectable kit. It was something she carried with her wherever she went. She told us not to worry. It was not as if something like this had not happened before. Epinephrine had always worked in the past, relaxing her lungs and keeping her breathing. True enough, but Lisette and I also knew that she would need time to fully recover – perhaps as much as a couple of days of rest. I could not help thinking about our plans to drive out from this small town early the next morning so we could be on our way back to the capital and from there fly to Tikal; and Tikal, as Lisette had reminded me, would probably turn out to be the highlight of the entire trip. I was concerned about Dominique – how could I not be concerned about her? – but I was also disappointed: a disappointment bordering on frustration. I paid the bill and the three of us waited for her to recover so we could walk back the hotel.

It did not, however, happen that way. It turned out that she had brought a second emergency epinephrine kit and she jabbed the needle into her arm.

It was then that a sense of urgency came upon us. We rose from the table and rushed out of the little restaurant. The way back to the hotel was obvious enough, even in the dark. I remember passing by the church – the men were still swinging their censers. It felt cold. Lisette and Edward were holding Dominique up and hurrying along.

I decided to run ahead so I could get help from the hotel in finding a doctor. The clerks behind the desk seem dazed. I started shouting. "I need a doctor ... take me to a doctor ... my daughter is in danger." I was aware of people looking at me strangely. I lost all sense of time. Finally a young man came up to me saying he would take me to where the doctor lived. By now the two of us were running. It could not have been very far. He led me to a small house inside a fenced-in compound. We were gathered up in darkness. The young man knocked on a door – nothing happened – but he went on knocking and in time a man did eventually come out. Yes, this was the doctor: youngish looking, a round unshaven face, with steel rimmed glasses and wearing a short-sleeved undershirt. I told him what was wrong. I must have been shouting, telling him whatever I could about my 19-year-old daughter – her allergies, her going into some kind of shock, her having taken a couple of doses of epinephrine. He also seemed stunned but then he reached for his coat and had the presence of mind to tell the young man accompanying me to rush back to the hotel and bring my daughter to the dispensary. The three of us ran down the narrow cobbled street. I remember the darkness and I remember thinking about how, during the course of my life, I had often watched distress and panic descend upon others while I had watched from the sidelines – concerned, perhaps, but safely detached from a reality that was not mine. Well, this time it was different. I was at the very centre of the anguish.

The dispensary cannot have been more than a couple of blocks from the hotel. Lisette and Edward were holding Dominique up. We carried her as best we could. The dispensary was open and the doctor heaved her onto an examination table. He filled her lungs with air, his hands joined together rhythmically pressing down on her chest. Lisette and I joined in with a hand pump fitted over her mouth. Edward was beside her. I have no idea how long all this went on for. I kept thinking that maybe we should have been injecting her with more epinephrine but that was not something the doctor seemed to think would make any difference; for all I know he did not even have epinephrine to give her. I kept looking at Lisette and Edward. I felt utterly helpless. I had never felt such helplessness.

Eventually, the doctor just stopped. He looked at us and said he was sorry. We had kept working well beyond the point of no return. There was simply nothing to say.

The doctor and his attendant moved us to a small room the walls of which were decorated with Mickey Mouse transfers: it was the part of the dispensary reserved for caring for children. In the silence of the night, a couple came up to us – I had not been aware of their presence. They were Americans who had followed us from the hotel. They hugged us and offered to call the United States Embassy in Guatemala City – there would surely be someone there to take care of emergencies: even late at night. There was, and the man at the other end of the phone told me he would take care of everything. He would have undertakers drive in from Guatemala City so they could pick up our daughter's body and have it flown back home. All we had to do was to stay with her – it would take them several hours to get to us.

I have never felt so grateful to utter strangers but then the pain set in. It was as if I was experiencing pain for the first time in my life. Intense pain is unsustainable. This was pain that swept over me in waves. It crashed down on me, raw and unforgiving – penetrating the depth of my being with the devastating reality that death is absolute and irreversible – and then it would recede like the tide only to return within a matter of minutes. Such anguish penetrates the body – it crowds around the throat, especially – bringing with it a dull, intractable ache. The tears press against the eyelids swelling them with the heaviness of distress.

My wife of over 20 years and my son now in his 15th year were beside me and yet the pain brought about utter loneliness: a helplessness rooted in the realisation that I could no more share in their own pain than they could in mine. A man came by. He offered to pray. What had he said? Lisette asked, not knowing Spanish. He had quoted John: "I am the way ... I am the resurrection." Hearing those familiar words did nothing to relieve my feeling of utter emptiness. It would have been easy to say that I was angry with God – assuming that at that point I even believed in his existence – but I was not really angry, I just felt utterly overwhelmed by pain. For the first time in my life I was experiencing unremitting helplessness. I half wished the man with the prayer had left us alone, but then he had the good sense not to stay, so I just thanked him. Only much later would I recall the good intentions of that total stranger with feelings approaching gratitude.

Every so often I would go up to the bed on which they had stretched out Dominique's body and touch her. Gradually, I became aware that warmth was slowly ebbing from her. I also felt cold, despairing and utterly vulnerable. The hours went by - my body shook and my teeth chattered - someone brought us hot tea from the hotel. There was a spare bed in the little room: Lisette thought it might be best for Edward to try to sleep, but I am not sure he was able to. The place was utterly still. I knew they would come to fetch her. It was an intensely anxious thought. It occurred to me that I was like a prisoner awaiting the inevitability of dawn - listening within the stillness for footsteps; footsteps that would stop outside my cell - thoughts so deeply recessed within the depth of my being that they were beyond sharing with anyone else.

Steps did eventually resonate within the stillness. They were the steps of men in dark suits that brought with them a grey metal box. They put Dominique inside it, but left it open. They had, they explained, called the municipality ahead of time so they could obtain a permit for the transfer of the body. Even though it was past midnight there were ways of taking care of such things. They would be back soon enough. Did we have special clothes for her? No, no, we said, she was wearing blue jeans and a thick comfortable sweater. That was good enough.

When they came back, they closed the lid and we walked behind the box out into the street where a small white van was waiting. We followed the white van on foot until it accelerated and disappeared into the night.

The night watchman let us into the hotel. I felt as if I was being observed; misfortune, I was to learn, has a way of inducing shame into the ones who suffer it. Before lying down beside Lisette, fully clothed and aching, I caught sight of an icon above the head of our bed - an icon in the style of the Indian artists of the colonial period. It was an image of Mary weeping at the sight of her crucified son. A sword pierced her heart: in fulfilment, I remembered, of the prophecy uttered by Simeon at a time of great joy. Mary had come into the temple, shortly after giving birth, to present her newborn child in thanksgiving.

16

Survival

Lisette and I were totally unprepared. How could it be otherwise? There was an outpouring of support. Lisette's brother, Richard Coghlan, immediately flew over to our home from England, as did others of our close friends. Dominique's high school friends rallied around us, especially around Edward. Dominique's closest friend, Lisa, was devastated. Lisette spoke to her mother in England at length over the phone, as I did to mine. Death sets in motion a sequence of events that confront the living with the need to make decisions, meet obligations and address concerns that are cloaked in the guise of business-like routine. Such is the emotional no-man's-land through which we made our way – tentatively and aware that our pain lay patiently in wait for us. The funeral, many said, was quite exceptional. Of course! The sudden death of a young person touches upon our deepest fears and evokes universal compassion. Dominique's friends eulogised her and formed a circle of support around Edward. Four years had gone by since my ordination as a deacon and the Catholic Church has its way of honouring and taking care of its own: in the solemnity of death, especially.

What to do next? How do parents deal with the gaping hole arising from the loss of a child? How do those whose suffering has set them apart from their fellow human beings reconnect themselves with the ordinariness of daily life? I stayed at home for a day or two following the funeral, but then just went back to work. I grabbed my briefcase, took the train into Manhattan and slipped back into my office hoping no one would notice that misfortune had overtaken me and that I was no longer the person I once was. The video production business Lisette had started up with a couple of partners was doing well and so, naturally enough, that is what she went back to. The Christmas vacation was over so Edward went back to school.

I do not know exactly how Lisette, and particularly Edward, felt. I could not. A truth that lies in wait for each of us to discover at some point in our lives is that pain is an intensely individual experience; it cannot be shared, still less understood by another – except perhaps by a compassionate god. If such a god does indeed exist this may well be his greatest gift to suffering humans.

It is quite true that nothing had prepared me to face the enormity of what had befallen us but, in one respect at least, I had been given the opportunity to learn something about suffering. Until my ordination I had not given much thought to what I might actually do as a deacon: the title itself is derived from a Greek word meaning service: service in some form to those in need.

Luckily, Father O'Connor, the priest in charge of the parish I belonged to was, in many respects, an unusual man. He had a gift for listening to and being present for those who faced a crisis in their lives: divorce, death, loss of livelihood and most especially sickness. He was not a stickler about upholding Church-made rules, especially when he deemed them to be in conflict with human needs. This, of course, made him unpopular with the powers-that-be, which in turn reinforced his popularity among those he cared for. He was the one who had suggested a few years before that I accompany him on a visit to the local hospital. I knew nothing about hospitals: to me they were unfamiliar, threatening places. I was largely ignorant of medical practice, the sight of blood made me queasy and I still had a primeval fear of corpses.

It happened on a Saturday morning. He had a winning way about him: those he visited knew that he cared for them unreservedly. He and I must have spent a good three hours together going from patient to patient – intensive care, cardiac care, emergency department, surgical recovery, general medicine, and on and on. At the end of it all he took me to the cafeteria and bought me a sandwich and a cup of coffee. 'That's it,' he said to me. 'I think you can do it. I'll make sure you get a badge.' I never turned back. He introduced me to the Hospital Chaplain, a Congregational minister, and she not only had a badge made for me but also took me under her wing and made sure I knew where to get help.

A year or so after that first visit to the hospital this holy man fell sick. It was a mysterious disease that laid him low within months. After his death some whispered he had died of AIDS. Maybe so! There was a time when the mere suggestion that such a thing was possible would have shocked me to the core, but life had begun to teach me deeper lessons. He was a profoundly caring priest who had passed something on to me that I would value for the rest of my life. I wished he had been physically present at Lisette's and Edward's and my side as we wept in that little room beside Dominique's body as the warmth of life went out of it.

I had also begun to better understand the mind-boggling complexity and confusion inherent within the human person – not to mention the suffering and the existential anxiety that goes hand-in-hand with that complexity. I was progressing toward my 50th birthday: how come it had taken me so long to confront some of these uncomfortable realities?

So, after Dominique's funeral, not only did I go back to work but I also returned to the hospital. I tended in those days to go there on Sundays. It was probably unwise for me to go back as soon as I did. How can someone listen to the suffering of a fellow human being when he is himself in a state of deep emotional shock? Unwise perhaps but not seriously so because, mystery of mysteries, I soon discovered what I already sensed; that concerning myself with the hurts of others seemed to pour balm over my own wounds. There was in fact less reason than ever for me to question the decision I had made in the hospital cafeteria some four years before. Visiting those in pain would, in time, become a source of significant support to me on my journey toward recovery.

On that flight back from Guatemala to New York I had begun to write. In a way, I had always wanted to write. My parents had made a living out of writing. Out of a desire to shake myself free of their misguided wish to mould me in their own likeness, I had shunned journalism and taken up a quite different career. I knew, though, that I could write; I had done so at Oxford and had gravitated towards a speciality within my profession that placed great emphasis on clear, concise written expression. My several efforts at writing a novel had, however, failed. It was the story-telling part of writing that was my weakness. I had never found anything really engaging to write about. Well, I thought to myself, as I sat between Edward and Lisette on that flight, aware of the tears that kept swelling my eyelids, now I actually have a reason to write. I have just lived though the most painful and intense hours of my life and, like it or not, I had an urge to write down exactly what had happened. I resolved to begin with the story of Dominique's death and of the day that had followed it. I sensed that this would be unspeakably painful but also felt, in a curious way, that I had no choice in the matter. Lisette was both encouraging and lucid: 'Do it,' she said, 'I can imagine that working for you. I'll help you and support you, but don't ask me to write anything. You and I are different.'

Our house in Greenwich has a winterised porch that faces east. In the winter, the morning sun streams in. It was a good place for our computer. I began writing as if my life depended on it: a couple of hours or so after a long workday in New York but above all at the weekends. The winter of 1989 was cold and I had little reason to spend time outside.

I started with the images that were haunting me: the long hours we had spent together on the night of Dominique's death in the little room in the deserted clinic with the Mickey Mouse transfers on the wall. But also something that had happened to me the following day that was especially painful to me. The three of us had driven back to Guatemala City early the next morning – a bright day that brought out the beauty of the highlands dotted with small cornfields and vegetable patches. We had gone straight to the American Embassy where a young African-American consular officer treated us with great kindness and competence. He took care of as much as he could but the three of us still had to visit the undertakers so we could choose a coffin – I paid for it with my American Express card. The consular officer had also asked to see Dominique's passport. When he gave it back to me it was stamped all over with CANCELLED in bold letters. Why was that so unexpectedly painful, I wondered?

Later in the day, the undertaker came by the hotel. He asked me to accompany him to the airport. I was too dazed to understand why. He took me to the Pan Am office in a hanger in the freight terminal. I was still dazed. Then I saw a couple of men heave a huge brown paper wrapped package over scales: they read out the weight and a third man sitting at a small desk wrote out a bill for me. Then I understood. I was devastated. I paid with travellers' cheques and the clerk gave me a few coins as change and a receipt. This was unimaginably painful. All I could think of was that they had given Judas a few pieces of silver. There was no logic at all to such a thought but that was what had come to me in the moment – it was the language of nightmares. I absolutely had to write all this down – urgently.

Should you not see a therapist, Lisette and I were asked repeatedly? Lisette did not want to, nor did I, really. We had come to this country from Europe: people of our generation only went to a psychiatrist if they were seriously sick. What about Edward? It might have been a good idea but neither Lisette nor I could speak for him. Later, maybe, but how could we tell? Is life not extraordinarily confusing at times? Anyway I kept writing. By then I had taken to computers. My firm had the wisdom to encourage everyone to use them – even older partners like myself who had been brought up in another era. I had an advantage, though. My father, hoping against hope that I would follow him into journalism, had given me a typewriter when I was about 16. I kept it in Normandy – no one in school or at Oxford would have dreamed of using such a machine – but had immediately taken to the clumsy old thing with its spools of black and red ribbons, teaching myself to use the keys without looking at them. So here I was writing about my daughter and saving everything on those funny looking 5 -inch floppy disks that were not always very reliable. In the office my secretary helped me out by backing up the files on to 3½-inch diskettes. I did not want to risk losing any of it.

I wanted to write about the days we had spent together on our vacation beside Lake Atitlán, gazing at the sunset behind the extinct volcanoes. These were the last days she had spent alive and so to me they were sacred. What other ways were there of preserving them besides writing about them? Preserving them for posterity? Perhaps, but that, I came to realise, is yet another illusion. So for love, I suppose. I had heard people say such things, but now I understood that this really was the only thing open to me. Yes, said Lisette, that is what it is, a labour of love.

How can anyone make sense of a world that allows a human life to be snuffed out before its appointed time? Appointed... by whom? Dominique was born at the Roosevelt Hospital in New York City on January 11, 1970. I wrestled with the absurdity of it all. She would have become a writer – a successful one no doubt since she really did have writing in her blood – but she had died a couple of weeks before her 19th birthday. Some kind person gave us a bunch of red roses on her birthday – it was a caring thought but I did not really know what to make of it. I was not prepared for any of this.

Did her short life have any meaning? There was a moment at which I would have willingly given up my own life in exchange for hers. Human beings are not generally given such choices but I really think I would have. Not that it would have been an easy thing to do. Even as a desperately wounded parent I still clung to my own life. And still do. That is the way we humans are. We are not heroes by choice. It takes a while to accept such a reality and I no longer think there is shame in such feelings.

In the days and weeks that followed Dominique's death, I was so numb that I lost my sense of taste, nothing seemed to matter any more. But then I began to recover ... the smell of fresh bread ... a kiss from my wife ... an engaging short story ... life has a way of reasserting itself. That is the way we humans are made but, yes, I am pretty confident that I would have given up my own life ... almost certainly but, to repeat, I had not been given that particular choice so all I could do was express my feelings.

What could I do? I could not bring Dominique back to life but I could try to gather together everything she had ever written ... or whatever I could get hold of. She was, after all, a writer and some writers live on beyond the grave thanks to the scraps of paper they leave behind. It is a tentative and shadowy way of surviving – not terribly real to those of us who survive for a while – but it is better than nothing: worth a try, I reasoned. I knew it would be painful, but pain had become a familiar companion.

So I went to work retrieving every notebook, every computer diskette, every scrap of paper I could find. After the funeral, Lisette and I had driven to Manhattan so we could collect whatever was hers out of the little room overlooking Broadway that she had shared with another Barnard student. There were term papers but also stories - mostly hidden in the recesses of computer diskettes - about meeting boys, singing at a candlelit Christmas concert in the Columbia University chapel, walking down Columbus Avenue late at night and arguing about Nietzsche, about the existence of God – questionable, at best – and about being gay. She was not, but had friends who were.

One piece stunned me. She had written about how one evening she had taken a few licks of an ice cream. I do not remember whether in the college cafeteria or at a party, but almost immediately she had felt her lungs clog and stiffen. A friend had helped rush her over to St. Luke's Hospital - just a few blocks away, next to the cathedral of St. John the Divine - and there she had waited in the emergency department, reflecting on the frailty of her existence, and then on how the shot of adrenalin she was eventually given had brought her back to life, for now at least. Much of what Dominique wrote was about her frailty, her awareness of death and her belief that life had to be lived with as much energy and intensity as it allowed.

Dominique never told us about her brush with death that particular evening nor with a similar incident that had occurred just a few weeks before and that she had also written about. She knew, as we did, that every incident involving anaphylactic shock exposes the allergic sufferer to greater risk the next time around: there is no build up of resistance within the body, quite the opposite. The ice cream must have had a trace of peanut mingled with it - for it was to peanuts that Dominique's physiology was so intensely allergic.

The hot chocolate drink she had ordered in the little restaurant beside the church with the white façade in Chichicastenango must also have had traces of peanut present within it. We never went back to find out: doing so would have served no useful purpose. I had, however, drunk what remained of it – she had taken but one sip – and to me it did no harm. I still live with the absurdity of that irony: it was a tepid, barely tasty, drink.

So, I went to work and, over the months, laboriously compiled an anthology of whatever she had written: there were poems, diaries, notebooks, articles – some published in local newspapers – but mostly just impressions jotted down. I would have been only too happy to make a book out of it – a book that would somehow have projected her life beyond the almost 19 years allotted to her. Wishful thinking, I suppose. She was possessed of the desire to write, did so with fluency, and had storytelling in her blood, but there was a huge hitch: she had only just embarked on the long road that would eventually make her into a professional writer. I was intensely moved by much of what she had written but I was her grieving father, not an objective reader. She was a talented and promising high school student but hardly a publishable author. So, I reasoned, maybe the task I should undertake is that of being her biographer: research as much of her life as I possibly can, tell her story in my own words and, whenever possible, quote from the rich source book of her own writings.

It turned out to be a far more extensive task than I had at first imagined. Until then, I had never kept a diary, nor had Lisette, and it turned out that our collective memories were woefully incomplete. Not just incomplete but worse: more like a jumble of anecdotes adrift in time and helplessly disconnected from each other. So I became a social historian, carefully reconstructing a 19 year time line, referring to whatever original documents were available to me and interviewing those who had known her. It became, as Lisette liked to put it, a labour of love, but also a painstaking work of social archaeology.

I worked intensely most evenings and weekends and after six months had put together a book-length document that was at least readable and coherent. It was a labour of love that confronted me with the disconcerting reality of how little I knew about my own daughter, of how much I had taken her for granted, and of the extent to which she, at times, viewed me as a controlling and insensitive father. These things brought their own particular pain. Dominique had also spent significant periods of time with my mother in the Normandy farmhouse to which I kept returning. Dominique's writing

1948 advertisement for The Fallen Idol, *in which my name is printed larger than top-starred Michèle Morgan and Ralph Richardson.*
(*by kind permission of David Rayner*)

IN THIS ISSUE : "THE STARS COME OUT" by DICK RICHARDS ("Sunday Pictorial")
PRODUCTION ARTICLE ON " QUO VADIS" by FRANCIS RAYMOND

The cover of ABC Film Review *in May 1952 following the release of* The Wonder Kid. *Filming began on picturesque locations in the Austrian Tyrol in September, 1949 but it wasn't given a general release in Great Britain until the summer of 1952. Since that time the film has completely disappeared; it has never been shown on television or released on video or DVD.*

(by kind permission of David Rayner)

At the age of 15 in 1954 with my beloved French grandmère in Normandy.

Lisette and I at our wedding in Kemerton, Worcestershire 1965

Our daughter Dominique pictured during our trip to Guatemala, just a couple of days before her death in 1988.

My mother with her dog Tessa, signing one of her books at the age of 96.

Edward and Dominque, pictured together in the summer of 1988.

Dominique and I with Ray Cabana (right) in 1988 with the poster my father had given me before his death in 1982.

Dominique and I in our house in Greenwich, Connecticut, in 1987. She was about to go to the High School junior prom.

This photograph of me was taken in 2013 outside the parish church of Saint Catherine of Siena in Greenwich, Connecticut, to which I have been assigned as a deacon since I was ordained in 1984.

(Photo: Bob Capazzo)

was also increasingly critical of my mother's limitations: particularly her failure to recognise that her desire to control her granddaughter was having a corrosive effect on their relationship. That was also painful to me.

Lisette was, of course, the first to read the manuscript. She had the good sense to realise that the labour of love that had brought it about had contributed to my survival and had almost certainly helped the two of us talk about our respective pain and keep our own relationship on an even keel. We had been warned that the loss of a child often places an unbearable strain on a marriage. It is, as I came to understand, the intense loneliness of each of the journeys that causes the bonds to strain and fray. Lisette and I were spared that particular additional misfortune.

I then showed the manuscript to Joe Mehan, a good friend who had stood by me during our ordeal. Many were the friends who had done their utmost to support us emotionally but Joe somehow stood out: at least as far as I was concerned.

Joe was a journalist who knew a good deal about writing but that was not the only thing that made him special to me. He had once been happily married with four young boys. One weekend he had unsuspectingly come home and been told by his wife she was leaving him for another man, leaving him looking after the boys and fending for himself as best he could. This was the 1960s, she told him, and such things were not unheard of. She had every right to embark on her own search for freedom and happiness and do so on her own terms. The suddenness of it all would have been a shattering experience for any caring man but in Joe's case the shock was particularly intense and devastating. He wrote a book about his ordeal and had no trouble finding a publisher. Those of us, I was to learn, who suffer a devastating loss feel the pain that results from it in our own particular way – it would also be meaningless to try to equate the pain of losing a child with that of a divorce – but the fact is that Joe had experienced intense pain and had undertaken to write about it. That itself was an act of courage. It had made him into the best of listeners. It is unrealistic to expect most people to really listen to the deep pain of a fellow human being. Understandably and naturally they shy away from it. It is just too uncomfortable. I suspect that self-preservation comes into play.

Joe read my manuscript and loved it: just the way it was, warts and all. He had friends in the publishing business and he exuded confidence. I was quite taken up by the idea of finding a publisher. Was I not still desperately in search of a means of prolonging Dominique's tragically short lifespan and finding meaning in both her life and in mine? Everyone was very polite, complimentary and sympathetic about the manuscript but there were no takers. Publishing is a business I was told, over and over again. It would be nice, those same people said, if there were a market for this kind of book but it deals with a subject no one really wants to go anywhere near. The loss of a child is, after all, the ultimate nightmare that haunts any thinking parent – to the point of being unmentionable.

At first, no one went so far as to bring up the literary shortcomings inherent in the manuscript. I knew, however, that there were plenty. I was not, after all, a professional writer. Then one of the publishers did mention the manuscript's shortcomings, and suggested I hire a professional to prune it and make it more palatable to a general reader. I was reluctant but, out of deference to Joe who thought it might work, I agreed to give the idea a try. The woman who worked up the text did so with professionalism and enthusiasm but it still did not work. I was disappointed, of course, not because I had put so much effort into this particular labour of love, but because it would have helped me cope with the immense sadness that my daughter had not lived long enough to see her name in print – to have the satisfaction of having something she had written actually published. That, at any rate, was what I thought at the time.

I put the two manuscripts aside, the original and the one that had been reworked. Even though more than 20 years have gone by, I have left them untouched. The loss of my daughter is still very present to me – the wound is no longer a bleeding open wound – but it is still there. The pain has a way of catching me unawares and of still reducing me to tears. I accept this with grace but I have no desire to make it any worse. What I have written here is, hopefully, more reflective and less raw than what I wrote then. It is also, hopefully, less threatening to a general reader. Lisette, Edward and I have survived those 20 years. I am still grateful to have had the courage to write what I did, to have kept talking about Dominique and to be able to say to this day how much I still miss her. Those things are in themselves significant achievements.

17

Exorcising The Spell

I have a vivid memory of being in my office one morning in the Exxon Building on Sixth Avenue and receiving a call from a man who introduced himself as one of my partners from an office in the Mid West. No more than a few months had gone by since Dominique's death. He and his wife planned to be in New York the following day. Would I be willing to join them for lunch? This had nothing to do with business, the man let on: someone had told him I had recently lost a child, so maybe I could help. He was particularly concerned about his wife.

At lunch, it was the man's wife who did most of the talking. It was about their son, a teenager. The young man had undergone a routine operation to have his tonsils out and been sent home the same day. The next morning she had found her son dead, his bedclothes soaked from the blood that had flowed out of the imperfectly cauterised incision. She was beside herself with grief. I just listened to the intensity of this woman's suffering, setting aside my own grief. She then said something that resonated within the depths of my being. She had feelings of guilt and shame. She had, she told me, taken to driving to the next town to buy her groceries. She had convinced herself that the check-out clerks in the local stores knew of her misfortune, and thought she should be ashamed of it. Why on earth should she have such feelings?

Why had I suggested to Lisette and the children that we eat an omelette in the little restaurant beside the church with the whitewashed façade? Why could we not have gone to the far fancier and more expensive restaurant in the hotel where we were staying? Why did I still feel guilt at having made that decision? And then why had I found it so difficult to walk back into the office on that first Monday morning after the funeral and face the embarrassed gaze of my work colleagues? Why had I felt like a wounded animal and why had shame mingled with that pain? I just listened to this grieving mother. In the moment of her telling it her story took on an intensity that eclipsed my own. What kind of world did we live in that a mother could be made to endure such suffering?

In the summer Lisette, Edward and I went to Europe, of course. We always had and would continue to do so. The summer before, Dominique had visited a number of Lisette's relatives and friends in England. She had, in particular, visited an old mill set in a beautiful spot in Gloucestershire. Lisette, as a young girl, had been to that very mill many times and, together with groups of friends, had played a daring game that consisted of jumping from one of the mill's windows into the dammed up river below. Dominique had done the very same thing, knowing she was following in her mother's footsteps and had described her feelings in her diary; one of the many documents I had painstakingly transcribed into my anthology of her writings. I asked Lisette to take me the mill. She did, and there we even met some of the people who remembered Dominique from the preceding summer. The sun shone brightly that day but what I remember most about it was the now familiar welling of tears behind my eyelids and the soreness in my throat. I was grateful, though, for I knew that this was yet another of the stages of the journey I had embarked on, and that at this point it was the only journey worth being on.

The Christmas holidays, our well-meaning friends had warned us, are times to be wary of. They were absolutely right about that. Dominique had, after all, died on December 29. Lisette and I resolved that, from that point on, we would do whatever it took to deflect as much of that Christmas misery as possible. It took courage to venture out so we could prove to ourselves we had the emotional wherewithal to resume doing what normal people took for granted. We took the first step the following year by accepting an invitation from close friends to visit them in Uruguay. The three of us took a Christmas day flight from JFK to Miami, hoping to continue on to Montevideo. Pan Am was still operating, but only just. We missed our connection and had a chaotic journey involving stopovers in Rio, the Iguazu Falls and Buenos Aires. It was enormous fun and staying with friends made all the difference. Lisette and I let the days run into each other hoping, unconsciously perhaps, that December 29 would go by unnoticed. It did, sort of. I remember with pleasure visiting a ranch in the middle of the pampas and sitting around a fire with a group of cowboys sipping mate tea from a shared pot. What really mattered, however, was that we were on the road to emotional recovery and that the good things of life were beginning to taste the way they once had. It would, nonetheless be a long road and one that we were still not strong enough to take on our own.

Lisette's brother Richard had, for some years now, been running a school in Herefordshire. Edward visited his uncle each summer and the two had developed a particularly close relationship. Why not, from now on, invite Richard to join us at Christmas time? That way he could spend Christmas with us and then be part of whatever short holiday trip we had planned for that year.

Richard's presence on those Christmas trips turned out to be immensely emotionally supportive to all three of us. So much so that one year Lisette had the courage to suggest that it might be a good idea to finish the journey Dominique's death had so tragically interrupted. I was at first terrified at the thought of returning to Guatemala but gradually came round to the realisation that all three of us were in need of some kind of exorcism.

Had our journey in the waning days of 1988 continued according to plan, Dominique, Edward, Lisette and I would have driven out of that little market town of Chichicastenango, returned to the capital to drop off our rental car and then taken a short internal flight to Tikal. Tikal is an extraordinarily rich 1,000-year-old archeological site set within one of the very few undisturbed stretches of tropical jungle left in the region. Miraculously, the conquering Spaniards and their successors paid it but scant attention. Tikal is the capital of a lost kingdom. It is a vast array of crumbling temples, terraces and dwellings in a dreamy, poetic setting reclaimed by and overgrown by nature. Dominique would have loved it.

Lisette figured out it was possible to get to Tikal by taking a short hop in a low-flying prop plane from Belize. This meant we would not have to subject ourselves to the emotional pain of going through Guatemala City. Belize is a small country carved out of Mexico's Yucatan peninsula by the British who during the 19th century were particularly covetous of its once abundant tropical hardwoods. The islands off Belize's Caribbean coast are surrounded by stunning coral reefs and this would have been reason enough for us to go there.

I do not think the three of us would have had the emotional stamina to make this trip on our own but, accompanied by Richard, we were prepared to give it a try.

The second morning of our stay, we rose an hour before dawn so we could hike to the base of the highest of Tikal's magnificent but decaying temples. We climbed it in the dark and then watched the sun rise over the jungle below – a vast, flat expanse of treetops emerging from the morning mist. Howler monkeys called to each other and parrots, flying in pairs and screeching, appeared in the first light. It was a magical moment and I remember being immensely relieved. We had finished the journey the four of us had begun. It felt to me as if we had a slain a dragon; the evil spell was no more; the pain, of course, was still there, but not the spell – there was a difference.

18

Looking Back On *The Fallen Idol*

It took me an extraordinary long time to look back on *The Fallen Idol*, that totally-out-of-the-ordinary event that intruded so powerfully into my childhood. When I say 'look back' I mean summon the courage and wisdom to exorcise it and, at long last, welcome it into my life. It was an event from which I was never fully able to escape. It would be an exaggeration to say it had haunted me – there was, after all, nothing even remotely horrific about it – it was just that it proved to be a surprisingly tenacious intrusion: it just would not let go and, like *The Hound of Heaven*, would be with me till my last gasp.

Today, at long last, I am able to look back at *The Fallen Idol* as something that was actually enriching and of which I am genuinely proud.

As a child everyone called me Bobby – Bobby in contrast to my father whose family had always called him Bob. When I married Lisette and went to America, I changed my name to Robert. I was quite deliberate about it but I could not, of course, change my name for those who already knew me: certainly not for my family, my wife, and my friends from the past. Let me just say, in retrospect, that this particular attempt to flee *The Fallen Idol* was only partly successful: a Google search of my name using Bobby yields a far richer and certainly more interesting crop than one using Robert. Too bad, but now I can at least smile at the irony of it all.

Lisette and I have lived almost all our married life in the United States. People, though, still occasionally ask us why we went there. I can offer an impressive number of excellent reasons. I am no exile. It is a country that has welcomed us and made us feel very much at home. I am proud to consider myself American and when I wrestle with the many problems that beset us as a nation I do so as one who is a member of the family. Perhaps though, when I suggested to Lisette almost a half century ago that we go to the US, I had an unconscious desire to put a little more distance between *The Fallen Idol* and myself? Perish the thought! I do admit, nonetheless, that at the time I relished the idea that such a move implied anonymity. That turned out to be yet another misplaced illusion!

Then why did I find myself earning my living as an accountant? Again, I can suggest plenty of fine explanations for such an outcome not least of which would be the ironical path so often taken by random events. If I were escaping from anything by making such a choice, it would far more likely have been the career in journalism that my father was so eager for me to pursue. But might it not have occurred to me – even if for the most fleeting of moments – that the accounting profession is a pretty good hiding place for an actor in search of a new identity? Probably, but even then I am not so sure. Years ago a friend gave me a cartoon cut out of the *New Yorker* magazine. There was this jovial, chubby, balding guy in shirt and tie sitting behind a big desk in an office. An earnest-looking journalist is interviewing him. 'Why did I give up being a film star? Oh you know it's the old story. I just got bitten by the accounting bug.' I am paraphrasing the caption because I had stuck the cartoon under a refrigerator magnet so I could get a chuckle out of it whenever I pleased. Unfortunately, it yellowed, eventually fell off, and just disappeared.

My accounting colleagues did not cooperate. They, along with my friends, both casual and close, kept telling me they had seen the film on TV: reruns, of course, and often late at night, but that did not stop them from coming up to me at the water cooler, at the supermarket, or even in church and saying they hoped I would not mind their asking but had they guessed right? Was I really the little kid in the film? They were polite about it, of course, and realised it was not something I wanted to talk about but that did not put them off. They got a kick out of it. They would ask me whether I was still earning royalties – money is one of the subjects that holds inexhaustible fascination for we humans. Alas no! I would exclaim with a wry smile – just a salary and rates of income tax well above 90 per cent: enough to dig my parents out of a financial hole and pay for my schooling. So it just would not go away. I thought that in time it would just wear off, and fade into nothingness, but actually quite the opposite happened.

When I did finally retire at the end of 1997 – I had reached the venerable age of 58 which in this particularly intense line of business is considered to be over-the-top – my work colleagues honoured me at a party at the Rainbow Room atop the Rockefeller Centre in the heart of Manhattan. It was a happy and elegant evening to which both Lisette and Edward were invited. I was, though, mercilessly roasted, as is the practice on such occasions. It was no accident that the entire roasting business was focused on *The Fallen Idol*. My friends had spared no expense in having a mock film made up highlighting my career with ample clips from the film. They had gone so far as to mount large posters on easels – there was the child, once again, looking down from atop the great marble staircase recreated inside Shepperton Studios some 50 years earlier. The fact is that everyone at the party wanted to be at last free to tease me. It was high time I let them do so. I marvelled, though, that once again the film had a life of its own.

A couple of years later my friend Nico del Castillo – who I suspected of masterminding that mock film at my retirement party – made me an unusual gift. Nico is originally from Uruguay and no year goes by without his returning to his native Punta del Este. It was thanks to Nico that Lisette, Edward and I had sipped mate tea with genuine cowboys on a Uruguyan ranch during the Christmas break of the year that followed Dominique's death. Uruguayans, so I'm told, have a fondness for classical films and it's apparently a good place to find the kind of memorabilia that film buffs so enjoy ferreting out. Nico had come across an embarrassingly elaborate – for me, that is – 28-page large format press kit produced for the launching of *The Fallen Idol* in North America. It was stuffed with effusive articles about this extraordinarily gifted child star – by then the marketing people had cottoned on to the idea that notwithstanding the stellar reputations of Sir Ralph Richardson and of Michèle Morgan it was the hitherto unknown child that the film-going public wanted to fuss over. The PR boys from the David Selznick organisation in New York City who were in charge of distribution had gone overboard with lurid posters, bombastic slogans and even catchy cartoons. I was grateful to Nico – of course, he's a wonderful friend – but also mortified. What? Mortified by this kind of bombast at the venerable age of 60! Yes, and so much so that I consigned it to the oblivion of the bottom drawer in our guest bedroom. Well now it is a good 14 years later, and I have allowed it out of the drawer and scanned it into my iPad so I can chuckle over it.

As I grew older I began to understand that those who knew me were puzzled that I shied away from talking about something that, as far as they were concerned, I should have been proud of. I began to reflect on this. Maybe it was that so public an exposure at a young age had induced in me feelings of vulnerability – feelings that others knew things about me over which I had absolutely no control and that this somehow left me unprotected. Then there was also this hard-to-explain feeling that because I had taken absolutely no part in the decision to act in the film, and because one of the explanations given for its resounding success was that Carol Reed – brilliant director that he was – had chosen a clueless child so he could control his every action, I was quite undeserving of all this fuss.

The great watershed of my life has, of course, been the death of our daughter Dominique. It has been an invitation to me to reframe all my feelings about the people I have known and the things that have happened to me from the very beginning. Curiously, it feels a little like resetting the clock: looking at everything within a more realistic, balanced context. So what *was* wrong about having been the star of a film? Why should I care about how it had come about? Why not just relax and enjoy it? Loss, after all, brings into sharp focus the overriding importance of enjoying and being thankful for what is capable of being enjoyed. Often the things that give us the most enjoyment are things we have chanced upon rather than worked for. Then the thought that being known as one who had starred in a film might expose me to some greater degree of vulnerability began to appear quite trivial – absurd actually – in the light of the change that the momentous event of the loss of Dominique had wrought within me. So maybe it was true that this film business had caused me over the years to wrestle with an event I wished had never happened, but why not now welcome such an experience? Is it not through such struggles, painful as they may be, that we learn about things that would not otherwise be within our reach? Should it not be our hope that each struggle prepares us in some way to better sustain those that will surely follow? Or maybe it was the other way round: that the truly momentous struggles help us appreciate the value of what the earlier ones had in them to teach us.

19

Further Bumps In The Road

Following Dominique's death my career as a tax consultant was to last another 10 years: years of relative stability, commuting to an office in Manhattan, caring for clients and working with younger colleagues. I learned to be grateful for the intellectual stimulation and for the friendships that came with the job. This looking back business does involve learning about the healing that comes about with gratitude. It was also a business that led me along a strikingly new path.

I had, over the 15 or so years that had gone by since my ordination as a deacon, developed a strong affinity for visiting the sick. There was nothing easy about hospital visiting but I had found it consistently emotionally engaging. It fed a part of my personality that was in need of nurturing. There was something emotionally grounding about it: an experience akin to prayer. It had been one of the lifelines thrown to me after my daughter's death.

So it was that, on retiring from my tax consulting career in late 1997, I decided to continue working - this time as a professional chaplain. Fifty-eight is a little late to begin a second career but the chance was worth taking. Some of my friends asked me tongue-in-cheek whether this was not really an attempt at a third career. Had I not, after all, been a film star? I just smirked.

People seeking to become chaplains do not, as I soon found out, have it easy. The first hurdle facing me was to find someone willing to train me - a hospital chaplain qualified to take on interns and, most importantly, in a position to put them out to work within the rough and tumble of hospital life. Interns typically work in groups of five or six; they visit patients and come back to their supervisor and to their fellow interns so they can reflect on their experiences. All this was very new to someone who had spent a career advising others on how to organise their affairs. Over the two years it took me to complete the training I joined four such groups in different hospitals: two of them – one in Manhattan and the other in Bridgeport, Connecticut – within the tough and often violent reality of the inner city. One of those summers, my job included being available to families coping with tragedies brought on by drug gang violence: there were dread calls from the emergency department in the early hours of the morning.

Two years to learn what, I was often asked. To listen might have been the short but accurate answer: to invite someone in the throes of pain and anxiety to speak about her emotional state as a means of better coping with her illness. Also, to overcome a natural inclination to give advice to those we visited. Why were we so ready to think of ways in which they might be rescued from the dire circumstances in which they found themselves and why on earth was this preoccupation with fixing things so very much at odds with our role as chaplains? This was what this whole thing was about: we have this primal need to be listened to and yet the world around us is so busy coming up with platitudes and ready-made solutions that we are left feeling lonely and neglected. Listening, as I was finding out, is hard work – such hard work that most of us are hard-wired to do everything within our power to shun it. It requires setting aside our own agenda and concentrating our entire attention on someone else. This listening thing came to be very much part of my journey.

There were also bumps along the journey that hit threateningly close to home.

One February evening in 1996 – I had not yet retired from my Manhattan-based consulting job – Lisette felt a lump in her breast. Once, many years before, the same thing had happened while we were in Washington just after our return from Singapore but it had turned out to be a false alarm. This time, alas, the biopsy was positive for cancer. Previous mammograms had failed to identify the emergence of several lumps that were now clearly identifiable in her left breast. They were not particularly large but the fact that there were several caused considerable alarm. Events moved quickly and we were advised to consider a mastectomy.

This was very hard news to bear. My first reaction was one of intense fear. Edward was still at college in Vermont, albeit in his senior year, and this was yet another jarring reminder of just how vulnerable our small family was to events wholly beyond our control. At a visceral level none of this seemed fair. Here we were once again faced with the possibility of an overwhelming loss. It had crept up on us, stealthily and then pounced with devastating suddenness. I had full intellectual awareness of the reality that there is no such thing as an inoculation against misfortune. I had seen plenty of cases during the course of my hospital visits where some new misfortune had struck people who had already had more than their fair share of suffering. It is one thing, however, to observe the misfortune of others – however empathetically – and quite another to experience them oneself. I was stunned and once more humbled. I missed my daughter terribly – with renewed intensity. Emotions build one upon the other.

Lisette, positive and cheerful as ever, took the news in her stride. The surgery was scheduled within a matter of days and we did our best to keep living as normally as possible. Following the surgery, the oncologists were optimistic. They made much of the fact that biopsies of nearby lymph nodes indicated the cancer had not spread. Notwithstanding the good news, Lisette was subjected to six months of chemotherapy. There is nothing easy about cancer. It is a particularly strident reminder of our vulnerability. Once present, it has a way of insinuating itself into the lives of those it has touched. It is ever present within the shadows. Our friends were unfailingly supportive. Cancer is, nonetheless, a persistently awkward subject for most of us to talk about. Most people would prefer to ignore it. 'Well she's cured now, isn't she?' I remember someone saying to me who should have known better. Lisette, thank God, is indeed a survivor.

My mother who in 1996 was still very much alive – she was only 90 at the time – had always had a great fear of cancer. When I started reading her books after her death in 2004, I learned of how her aunt – my beloved grandmother's elder sister – had died in her 40s of a particularly virulent and painful form of uterine cancer. This loss had made a deep impression on my mother. That may, I now think, have made it particularly difficult for her to deal with what had befallen Lisette. She did not want me to speak of the cancer to any of her friends. I was once more up against this mysterious and seemingly irrational feeling that misfortune is something to be ashamed of, something that is somehow connected with a sin committed by the victim or by those close to her. That I now realise is something the author of the Book of Job had observed in human behaviour. It was something I had experienced for the first time after Dominique's death.

As my mother aged into her 90s, I became increasingly concerned with caring for her and that turned out to be a bumpy road indeed and some of the roughest bumps were the unexpected ones.

On that summer vacation to Europe following Dominique's death, Lisette and I had gone to Normandy. There I had seen Dominique everywhere. How could it have been otherwise?

I spent several hours one afternoon in the little half-timbered barn at the edge of the garden. It had once been a bake house and, for all anyone knew, just like the farmhouse, dated back to the 16th century. As a child, I had spent many happy hours tinkering and daydreaming here and I knew Dominique had done the very same thing. It is a meditative, prayerful kind of place. That afternoon I sat on a folding chair beside a large wooden box we had long ago used for storing potatoes. Out of curiosity I peeked inside and there, quite by chance, found a school exercise book. I immediately recognised Dominique's writing. She had written about how hard it was for her to cope with my mother's insistence that she continue to conform to her expectations – expectations rooted in my mother's vision of Dominique as the little girl who had worn pretty dresses and charmed her grandfather with her precocious intelligence and eagerness to please.

Dominique had experienced her grandmother as being quick-witted, a gifted observer of other people's foibles and weaknesses and irrepressible when it came to speaking her mind, the consequences-be-damned. She had not earned her reputation as a writer for nothing.

Dominique was right: my mother did hold others to standards that were unrealistic and yet, when she chose to, she could be charming, engagingly affectionate and a source of comfort for those in need of emotional support. As powerful as such attributes might have been for a storyteller and for a writer, they were not conducive to harmonious relationships.

Dominique had visited her grandmother one last time before beginning her first year at university. Sadly, it had not been a happy visit. No sooner had Dominique arrived than she asked her grandmother to drive her to the station so she could take a train to Paris: ostensibly to spend a weekend with a girlfriend. My mother was offended. She had been looking forward to spending as much time as possible with her granddaughter. Dominique came back from Paris sooner than expected and it transpired that there was no girlfriend. She had, in fact, arranged to see a boy she had met on the beach the previous summer. My mother need not have worried – they had not hit it off, hence Dominique's precipitous return – but she felt her granddaughter had double-crossed her, and resentment set in.

My mother knew that my daughter's death had wounded me within the depth of my being and she also was wounded, but differently. My mother kept saying things I did not want to hear. 'Had your daughter lived, she would have caused you much anguish. She was far too wilful ... far too independently minded.' I was a wounded child and I also had unrealistic expectations: mothers are supposed to nurse their children until their hurt goes away. That is a need we do not apparently grow out of. My mother and I were, in fact, on separate paths - deep grief does that kind of thing to people. It does horrible things like break up marriages. My mother was not always likeable but I loved her and so very much wanted to find a way of healing this threateningly painful rift. The healing did come about but it took time - much longer than I would have wished.

As I learned to listen better to my mother, over the years that followed Dominique's death, I also came to understand that she was still grieving over the loss of her two-year-old brother - something that in a mysterious way had contributed to the separateness of the paths we had taken in dealing with our respective losses. That, of course, was the very loss that, in the light of Dominique's death, had drawn me so intensely to the memory of my beloved grandmother. We had both lost a child.

The seemingly inconsequential story about Dominique tricking my mother into driving her to the railway station so she could meet up with an old boyfriend turned out to be an unexpectedly powerful parable about just how hard it can be to come to terms with unrealistic expectations. It scarred for the longest time my relationship with my mother - it shouldn't have but it did.

It became increasingly necessary for me to make regular visits back to the ancient house of my birth. I did so four, sometimes five times a year. These were short visits during which I enjoyed my mother's company. She had a remarkably engaging personality and was determined to keep up with current affairs. She kept asking me questions about the state of the world and was never without a book: novels, histories and, most of all, biographies.

My mother missed my father acutely and to her great credit never failed to attribute her success as a writer to his persistence and mastery of the English language. She did, nonetheless, take great pride in what she had achieved. The other thing she talked about frequently and predictably was *The Fallen Idol*. She made no bones about having basked in the limelight of it all. She had been the mother of the star, had her 'director's' chair on the film set with her name etched in its canvas and she was the one the press had turned to for interviews during the heyday of the film's success. We always spoke in French so it was '*le film*' she invariably spoke of nostalgically and effusively. The film business apparently brought with it a great deal more glamour and limelight than the ancient trade of storytelling. Looking back, of course, it now occurs to me why I found all this film chatter rather irksome - I was still in my ostrich phase.

During the summer months it was not unusual for total strangers who had read her books to drop by the ancient farmhouse unannounced. They were greying Brits, mostly, but also a handful of Americans. My mother referred to them as her 'fans', complaining loudly that they were unwelcome intruders. She was, in fact, hugely flattered at the thought that people were still seeking her out.

The fact is that my mother's visiting fans were invariably delighted by the quaintness of the house and by the way she chose to live; surrounded as she was, by a chaos of her own making. My mother, if she happened to be in good mood, invited her fans into her kitchen - the inner sanctum - and gave them a cup of tea. She could be engagingly charming. She addressed her fans in her fluent but strongly accented English and, because she was increasingly deaf, found it convenient to do most of the talking. They could not fail to be impressed by the strangeness of her surroundings. My mother had, since my father's death, become a hoarder. She had the greatest difficulty throwing anything away - newspapers, boxes, worn out clothing - and she had lined the walls of her kitchen with a great assortment of cards, hand-written lists made on the reverse of cereal boxes - my mother was not one to waste paper - and photographs and pictures cut out of magazines of anything and anyone that caught her fancy ranging from cute kittens to the Queen of England. Having run out of wall space, she had taken to dangling cards from strings slung across the kitchen and tied to hooks on opposite walls. She thought nothing of screwing her hooks into whatever piece of furniture might be in the way, or into the ancient house's timbers. The cards were secured to the strings with wooden clothes pegs. A childhood memory of an illustration in a book of nursery rhymes of *The Old Lady in the Shoe* kept popping back to mind.

The other thing about my mother that never failed to impress visitors was her keeping of chickens. She was devoted to her chickens, each had a name and she often reminded me that they - together with her small sausage dog and ginger cat - were her true children. 'I find affection wherever I can,' was the way she often put it to me. At night the chickens perched in what had once been the stables, a short walk from my mother's back door along a concrete path. Rain or shine, the first thing my mother did each morning was to shuffle over to the stables in her rubber clogs, hunched over, and holding onto her cane. She would open the stable door and give them what she referred to as their breakfast; a homemade hotpot the principal ingredient of which was chunks of stale bread soaked in warm milk.

My mother's mind remained sharp as ever: not just sharp, but also sharp edged. When I was young, I imagined that one of the good things about ageing was that it was a time to be mellow. People who are mellow, it seemed to me then, must also be wise and serene. I was wrong. I had failed to take into account having to deal with loneliness, the humiliation of physical decay, diminishing expectations and plain old anxiety. My mother had always been highly-strung and prone to fits of anxiety. Old age does not do away with such character traits.

My mother did things and said things that were not just outrageous but also, at times, extremely funny. She still drove around in a vintage two horsepower Citroën – the quintessential post-war French car with a lawnmower-sized engine and bouncing springs, thus keeping up the pretence she was capable of doing her own grocery shopping. The ancient house was only a mile from the centre of town, but for my mother it was a risky journey down a steep hill. She was deaf and her short-sightedness had intensified. People heard her coming from afar and kept their distance. She routinely ignored stop signs and the police had tried to take away her licence but the judge hearing the case had taken pity on her: old ladies in their 90s making a go of driving around in a two-horsepower Citroën deserve some respect. She did command respect and to this day there are people in the village who refer to me as 'the son of the lady in the Old Citroën'.

I jotted all this down and there was enough material to fill several notebooks: her attempts to protect her chickens from marauding foxes; her erratic relationships with the small group of friends that stood by her against all odds; the chaos resulting from her reluctance to throw anything away; and the unrealistic demands she made of the farmer whose cows grazed the few acres of farmland my father had acquired over the years. Those were the whimsical and endearing things about my mother.

My mother lived into her 98th year, and her wish that she never be confined to a nursing home was granted. Early one morning in mid-April 2004 the telephone rang in Greenwich while Lisette and I were still asleep. My mother had fallen on the way back from the chicken coop, inside the house fortunately, and outwardly only bruised. A neighbour who luckily had dropped by that morning had found her. The disagreeable truth was that my mother could not get up from the chair into which she had been lifted. There was no choice but to call an ambulance. They took her to the local hospital, and at first she did well. She was alert enough to worry about her dog and her chickens.

The early morning call was from the hospital. The nurse I spoke to was reassuring and I told her I would be on my way. Within 48 hours Lisette and I were at her bedside. She immediately recognised me and told me she was glad I had come because she was now well enough to be taken home. 'I'm tired of this place,' she said, 'get me out of here!' That was quintessentially my mother. Then, within minutes, she fell silent, and never spoke again. She was moved to a room of her own and the nurses helped set up a cot for me so I could sleep beside her. I could tell from the intermittent rhythm of her breathing that she was near death: so could the doctor who suggested we do nothing except keep her comfortable with a hydrating intravenous drip. He thought she might have had a series of strokes but, wisely, recommended against doing any kind of test or scan. 'We don't really need to know, do we?'

At dawn, at the end of the third night I had spent beside her, I noticed she had stopped breathing. She had been granted her wish.

20

The Survivors

The closing months of 2001 turned out to be awesomely eventful. I had, by then, joined the staff of the local hospital. It was a Tuesday morning in early September. I was paged and the switchboard operator told me it was an emergency. Would I go to the oncology unit? I recognised the room number. It was a patient I had visited several times before. She had spent time in intensive care and I remembered her well. She was in her late 40s, originally from England, and her husband was a kind, caring man. The moment I walked into the room I realised she had just died. Her husband was at her bedside. I went up and hugged him – there was nothing to say. I took his wife's hand and knelt beside him. The room was quiet. 'A prayer?' I asked after a while. 'Yes,' he whispered. The prayer was brief and familiar; said slowly. I squeezed his hand and then slipped out of the room.

In the hallway I overheard a nurse say a plane had crashed into the World Trade Centre. My emotions still focused on the immediacy of death, an image came to mind: of a confused and hapless pilot who had crashed his frail propeller-driven plane into the great steel mass of a building I was quite familiar with. Had I not, over the many years I had worked in Manhattan, often had occasion to take one of its astonishingly fast elevators all the way to the 120th floor? There were, all the way up there, classrooms in which up and coming executive types would gather to learn about the finer points of business practice. Every so often I would go up there to teach a course on international tax – that was in a prior life!

Calmly, I walked over to the general medical unit on the floor below for my next visit. The next thing I remember was a call to me by an elderly woman – she was a patient watching TV from her bed. 'Come look!' she said, with a sense of urgency. It was then that I saw one of the towers crumble into a billowing mass of black smoke. 'Do you know that this is the second tower to come down?' she asked me. How could I have known? My mind was still in that room where a husband was watching over his young wife's lifeless body.

Something else happened that year – embarrassingly banal, really, but that to me turned out to have a far-reaching influence. The British Film Institute had contacted me, an organisation I had never heard of. The BFI, I was told, not only sponsors a large-scale international film festival in London each November but it had also funded a 're-mastering' of *The Fallen Idol*. A re-mastering? That's apparently akin to the restoration of an antique: repairing and refreshing the best available copy of a classic film so it can be rereleased for distribution and also issued for the first time in digital format. Would I be willing to fly to London so I could attend the first public screening of the re-mastered print, be interviewed, and talk to the press?

How on earth had the BFI tracked me down? Through my mother, apparently, whose French address was still in *Who's Who*. I surprised myself by how easily I had accepted the invitation. Why ever not? Besides, this business of having to care for my mother involved me in making frequent trips to Europe.

Of the many people involved in the making of the film in 1947 only four, I was told, were still alive. Out of that four, three of us had accepted the invitation to be guests of the BFI: the other two being Guy Hamilton, Carol Reed's assistant director, and Dora Bryan, now in her 80s who had played the young hooker in the police station scene. Only Michèle Morgan, also in her 80s and leading a secluded life in France, had declined.

I had flown to London not knowing what to expect and without giving the matter much thought. All I knew was that there would be a dinner, a screening of the re-mastered copy of *The Fallen Idol* – it looks gorgeous, I had been told over the phone – and that I would be asked to join the other two survivors on the stage so as to answer questions from the audience.

That is pretty much what happened. The theatre was packed and there were even autograph hunters – a persistent and pushy breed that caught me unawares. They knew exactly what they wanted. Please sign as 'Bobby' many asked. I did, dutifully. I was past fighting this thing. I was given a felt tip pen and instructed just where to sign over glossy, gloriously sharp black-and-white prints of close ups taken 53 years before and reproduced by the BFI for the benefit of film buffs. For me it was the oddest of moments: the film had come out in 1948 and here I was in 2001, still alive and at last able to reflect on this most curious of happenings.

The answering of questions on the stage – or what turned out to be the interview of the survivors – marked a turning point. This was the first time I had ever been asked as an adult, and in public, to reflect on my acting past. From then on I would look at *The Fallen Idol* in a new light.

I was asked to what extent the child that I was had awareness of the emotional import of the story at the time of the filming. I replied that it should be fairly obvious that at the age of eight I was hardly in a position to do so. What I did not admit to, however, was that I was only just then embarking on my own voyage of discovery in relation to the film. I had not, for example, yet read Graham Greene's *The Basement Room*: a glaring omission attributable no doubt in very large part to my carefully nurtured ostrich-like attitude. All my life I have been an avid reader. I had even studied literature. When it comes to storytelling I take great enjoyment in reflecting on the technique used by a writer to achieve a particular effect. Was it not high time I begin reflecting on the aspects of the human condition Graham Greene was wrestling with when he wrote the story?

Eureka! The telling of the story through the eyes of a child is, of course, a literary device: one readily transposable to film. The primary purpose of such a device is for the child to act as a lens through which the reader – or in this case the audience – is invited to view the events as they unfold. The purpose of a lens is to bring into sharper focus truths that might not otherwise be apparent to the audience. The presence of the child is revelatory. It could also be said that the lens – like a light angled in a particular way – is what enables the author to bring out the aspects of the story that are of particular concern to him. Such an analogy presupposes that the lens is an instrument: an instrument carefully and skilfully crafted by both writer and director, but no more than an instrument. It therefore made enormous sense for those involved in making the film to choose a child who not only had not reached the age of self-reflection but who also had no prior acting experience.

What struck me that damp November evening in London is that I should no longer deny myself the pleasure of looking at the entire *Fallen Idol* experience through the eyes of an intellectually curious observer: an observer no longer encumbered by superfluous emotional baggage. It was as if I had decided to wipe the lens clean and, at long last, use it as directed. I could now be the grown-up viewer looking through the child's eyes: as they were then, unencumbered. That would turn out to be the best of exorcisms.

The dinner prior to the screening turned out to be equally momentous. No, not what we were served: a perfectly harmless sliver of chicken breast with a few sprigs of lettuce on the side and a slice of cherry pie. The momentousness had to do with being among the survivors. There was Guy Hamilton. I am embarrassed to admit that that evening I knew nothing about Guy Hamilton beyond the fact he had been Reed's directorial assistant and that he was still alive. The truth is that I had no memory of him. I do not mean that to be a put down. Far from it! There are plausible reasons for such a lacuna. Carol Reed was so meticulously driven a producer that he was personally involved in every scene. That did not leave much scope for an assistant except to perform background tasks that, however essential, would have had little visibility. Why, though, do I have such clear memories of all the actors and not of Hamilton? I have come to believe that most memories are composites, added to through retelling and through successive exposure to images. I remember the actors so well probably for the simple reason that, over the years, I have had occasion to see the film once in a while: thus reinforcing and layering those particular memories. The young, also, are adept at viewing the world within a narrowness of angle that suits their self-centredness: we are all good at doing that but the young excel at it.

I should, of course, have looked up Hamilton on the Internet or at the very least asked my hosts at the British Film Institute to provide me with his biographical details. They would have done so willingly. Here is what I should have known about the man I sat across from that evening.

Carol Reed liked his work and had taken him under his wing. Not only was Hamilton also Reed's assistant for *The Third Man* but, in certain scenes, he also subbed for Orson Welles. Nothing shabby about that! Then Guy Hamilton went on to direct films of his own: lots of them as it turned out but, surprise of surprises, three of the notoriously spoofy James Bond films everyone, including myself, had enjoyed so much. The James Bond film series, based on Ian Fleming's successful spy yarn fantasies, was launched in 1962 with *Doctor No* and quickly followed by *From Russia with Love* (1963). Hamilton's opportunity came the following year when Terence Young, who had directed the first two in the series, stepped down following a pay dispute. Hamilton was asked to direct *Goldfinger*. It turned out to be the biggest, splashiest, and probably best known of the Bond films. According to the critics, Hamilton seemed to have had a knack for coming up with the right mixture of gorgeous girls, tongue-in-cheek use of over-the-top gadgetry, and outrageously exaggerated chase and combat scenes. This was the film that starred the Aston Martin with the ejectable seat, the gold-painted seductress – in the nude, of course: and the kinetically supercharged duel-to-death inside Fort Knox – gold bars, glistening in the background.

Then there was Sean Connery in the role of James Bond – actually Sir Sean Connery since he was knighted in 2000.

Hamilton went on to direct another three of the films in the series, *Diamonds are Forever* (1971) with Connery once more playing Bond, and then two others with Roger Moore in the lead role: *Live and Let Die* (1973) and *The Golden Gun* (1974). Not only was I in blissful ignorance that I was being interviewed that evening together with the man who had directed Sean Connery in the most successful of the James Bond films, but it also strikes me now as decidedly odd that when I saw *Goldfinger* back in 1964, and loved it, it never crossed my mind that I might have had a connection with its producer. Some aspects of my ostrich-like behaviour had obviously been only too successful.

What do I remember of Hamilton from the interview that had brought us together after a lapse of more than 50 years? I took from it the clear message that he did not have warm memories of the child it had been his boss's job to direct: a brat, no less, too bright and restless for his own good, and impossibly distractible. Those are my words. Hamilton was polite enough not to voice his feelings quite as starkly, but he made no bones about saying that without Reed and without his own personal efforts I would have been a complete wash out.

I was mildly peeved by Hamilton's attitude toward me that evening. It was to be followed by something that I found considerably more irksome. The BFI had a vested interest in raising awareness of the availability of *The Fallen Idol* in its re-mastered form. The film critic of *The Guardian* – one of the few remaining British daily newspapers with any kind of intellectual standing – was interested in doing a piece on the film and had asked for an interview. I, naturally enough, agreed to it and remember the interview itself over breakfast in my hotel as being quite unremarkable. During it, however, I was not aware that Hamilton would also be interviewed for the same article. In the published article Hamilton was quoted as saying: 'Bobby had the concentration of a demented flea, Carol and I would play good cop, bad cop. I could shout at him, but Carol could never lose his temper, even though the sweat would be pouring down his face. He would film six or seven hundred feet of film just to get one line'. Much of the article continued along the same lines with Hamilton making the point that it was thanks to the work done in the cutting room – where he presumably played a key role – that the film was salvaged. Hamilton is also quoted in the article as describing me as 'an odd little boy, quite effeminate ...'

What did reading the article feel like? It made me angry. Hamilton, I reasoned, was well within his rights to express his dislike of me but I in turn could not help feeling that his views were biased: a bias that must surely have come from the fact that when the film came out the critics and the audiences just loved the little boy - he stole the show. He still does! That must have peeved Guy Hamilton no end. Too bad! And too bad for me because the article also reminded me of those feelings of vulnerability I had experienced as a child when, having been dragged into this business without having had any say in the matter, I had no choice but to submit to the intruding gaze of the multitude. What I had now finally come to terms with is that it made no sense to pretend the thing had never existed. That November 2001 visit to London brought home to me the reality that it was time to cast aside the ostrich policy and come out of that particular closet by just telling my story. My astute wife also remarked that it was little wonder that my eight-year-old brain had been washed clean of any memory of Guy Hamilton. He admitted in the article, she pointed out, to being the bad cop - that's a very forgettable role!

Had I known about *Goldfinger*, I would most likely have made an effort to bridge at least some of the distance that separated us that evening but that was not to be. It would also have been helpful to me to know that we did have something in common: we were both born in France and brought up speaking French, although in his case both his parents were English. He was born in 1922 and so he is some 17 years my senior. He is, so far as I know, still alive and retired. Incidentally, so is Connery, living in the Bahamas and still making money - which I cannot believe he can be in need off - by posing as a handsome, but now ageing, roué in a hammock wearing a cocked hat and doing all this on behalf of Louis Vuitton luggage.

I have a diametrically opposed impression of my meeting, that evening, with Dora Bryan. To begin with she was the only person connected with *The Fallen Idol* that I had actually come across after the making of the film: that highly contrived *This Is Your Life* encounter in a BBC studio when I was still in my early 20s. But above all I remembered Dora from the days of the filming. Hers was a very minor and unessential role but it stood out. She put in the kind of act that grabs audiences and delights YouTube fans. Carol Reed had a gift for inserting seemingly gratuitous clips into a narrative mainstream and they were invariably humorous and ironic. This one was not part of the terse story line of *The Basement Room* but I can imagine Graham Greene warming to Reed's suggestion that it be sneaked into the script. It comes at a turning point in the story. The child, seeing the butler's wife's body come to rest lifeless at the bottom of the staircase and, thinking she had been deliberately pushed over the banister by the butler - his hero - escapes terror-stricken into London's darkened streets. Eventually, rescued by a policeman, he is brought into the local station but there stubbornly refuses to talk. Nothing the police do can make the child say where he is from or what has made him run away from home in the middle of the night. Enter Rose: she has just been arrested for soliciting, she's a regular and the police know her only too well. There is something, though, about Rose that draws people too her. Before long the child is sitting on her lap, sipping a huge mug of hot tea. 'Where does your dad work?' she asks. 'He doesn't work,' I reply, 'he's the ambassador'. Funny enough, but then comes the line that brings the house down - the funniest in the whole film - Rose says it impishly and enthusiastically in her best cockney: 'Your dad's the ambassador! Oh I know your dad!"

Someone asked me if at age eight I knew what a hooker was. Probably not, but in a vague kind of way I might have. Children are intuitive. The fact is it did not matter one bit. The audience was being invited to see the scene through the eyes of a bemused child and they loved it: that is what literary genius is all about. Good for Carol Reed and good for Graham Greene!

That was Dora Bryan heavy with lipstick and in a gaudy, shiny raincoat in the role of Rose. She was only 24 at the time and already established in what would turn out to be a remarkably long and successful career as a character actor in countless supporting roles on stage, screen and TV. Audiences loved her and warmed to her outgoing personality.

On that November evening in 2001, Dora was now 78 and still working hard. I wished I had known then some of what I now know about her, but maybe it would not have made any difference because we immediately bonded. She struck me in many ways as a very fortunate person: fortunate because she had achieved professional success, was admired and loved by everyone who had ever met her, and had committed herself to a life-long loving marriage. Her life, however, had also been extraordinarily painful.

Those of us who have lost a child somehow just know when we are in the presence of someone capable of listening to our story. That is exactly what happened at dinner. I cannot remember which of us first spoke of it, but out it came. She told me she had lost her daughter. Her name was Gina, she was 36, an alcoholic and that is what had caused her death. I am invariably stunned by such stories: they all seem to be so much worse than mine. I might have know about this had I had the presence of mind to get hold of Dora's life story before flying to London but I had not and so for me it just came out of nowhere. The story of my own loss of my daughter Dominique likewise came out of nowhere. How could she imagine that the sweet eight-year-old blond child she had propped up on her knees in a studio-built police station smelling of plywood and fresh paint would one day grow up and experience something like this?

When, much later, I set about writing this book, I was particularly anxious to find out more about Dora. She had perfected a knack for comic parts. In 1963 she immortalised a wildly zany song called *All I Want For Christmas Is A Beatle* that remains a YouTube favourite, and in 1966 delighted British audiences playing the prissy headmistress in one of the silliest films of all time *The Great Saint Trinian's Train Robbery*. She is also a highly respected actress. It was none other than Noel Coward who picked up on her ability to master character parts and in the mid-1940s cast her in a revival of *Private Lives*. In 1996 she won the Laurence Olivier award for playing in Harold Pinter's *The Birthday Party*.

She is still alive but sadly confined to a wheel chair, afflicted by dementia and living in a nursing home in Hove. Hers is a heart-wrenching story that one of her empathetic biographers described as a catalogue of unimaginable disasters. There was first and foremost the death of her daughter but also recurring struggles with debilitating mental breakdowns, and with alcoholism. Then for years she and her husband took care of their oldest son who was afflicted with a painful disease involving chronic inflammation of the spine. She also suffered financial ruin from a co-investment with her husband in an ill-fated hotel venture. Finally her husband, who as a young man had played professional cricket, died of Alzheimer's.

I read somewhere that, following her daughter's death, Dora would greet the new moon by bidding her daughter Gina good night. That makes sense. We do things like that. It helps us survive.

When I worked as a hospital chaplain people often confided in me that they felt life had not been fair to them. Was it OK to be angry with God for tolerating such unfairness in a world he had apparently created? I never had it in me to contradict them. Yes, it's OK. If God does indeed exist then he's up to dealing with our anger! I am a Catholic but I still struggle with the limits of how far faith will take me every day of my life.

21

Through Grown-up Eyes

By accepting the British Film Institute's invitation to come to London at the end of 2001, I had taken the first step toward abandoning the pretence that *The Fallen Idol* had never happened and, on the contrary, welcoming it into my life as an enriching experience worthy of being nurtured.

On my return from London I undertook something that those more attuned to psychotherapy than I am would surely regard as significant. In the years leading up to his death my father, knowing he had a weak heart, had made a point of gradually handing over to me objects he valued and wanted me to care for. Many of these were books to which he had grown emotionally attached. Some he wanted me to hold in safekeeping for my daughter Dominique and those he often accompanied by a note – a sticky label, a scrap of paper, a dedication – addressed to her directly beginning with the words 'My dear princess'.

He died in 1982 and she in 1988.

Whenever I run my hand along the bookshelves in our living room and find myself holding one of these books, that familiar pain – the tightening of the chest, the constriction of the throat, and the swelling behind the eyelids – returns with a swiftness that is its very own.

My father also gave me a large brown envelope containing a folded up two-and-a-half by four foot promotional poster of *The Fallen Idol*, colour tinted but cheaply printed on newspaper quality paper. The commercial artist, though, had done a fine job and what my father must have liked about this particular poster is that it features a head and shoulders portrait of the child drawn against the background of the famous staircase at the foot of which the butler's wife's body had come to rest. The names of the principal actors are blazed across it and mine is there very, very slightly larger than that of Ralph Richardson and Michèle Morgan. The earlier posters, I later found out, relegated the unknown child's name to an inferior and decidedly smaller segment. The success of the film, increasingly attributable to the unusually engaging part given the child, had changed all that – the publicity people had seen to it. So it was only natural that my father should have selected one of the later posters. He attached to it one of his sticky labels and this one was addressed to me. 'Varnish it,' he instructed me, 'and make sure the frame is simple but well made.' I had taken the envelope home to Connecticut and put it out of the way in the very same bookcase in which I had stacked the books I would never be able to pass on to my daughter.

The envelope had lain there over 20 years. The time had come to rid that old poster of its creases and of the acid that had yellowed and made brittle its flimsy paper. It has now been preserved and framed and hangs prominently in our kitchen – everyone comes through our kitchen – and visitors cannot help noticing it. They ask me questions. I am perfectly happy for them to do so. I, in fact, welcome it. Do I not have every reason to be proud?

Then one February morning in 2006 I received a phone call from a man in New York who explained he was in the film distribution business. Did I know that *The Fallen Idol* was being shown at the Film Forum on Houston Street? Did I know anything about his company Rialto Pictures? This enterprising man must have known I do not react well to strangers who call me cold, because he had sent me a Film Forum poster – with my picture on it, of course – and a letter by express mail. I was surprised when the UPS man knocked, but then so was the man from Rialto who called me because he clearly did not know what to make of someone who was a Catholic deacon. Most people do not, I told him, reassuringly. Would I consider taking the train into New York so I could have dinner with him and his business partner and then answer questions after a showing of the film at the Film Forum? Would my wife mind coming along... even my son?

This was Bruce Goldstein who, in the late 1990s, had started up a film distribution business specialising in the many once famous classics that were still fabulous but had for one reason or another fallen off the commercial merry-go-round. It had turned out to be an inspired idea. I liked lots of things about Bruce, beginning with his enthusiasm and his scholarly interest in the films he chose to promote. Had I read Graham Greene's *The Basement Room*, had I read such and such an article, had I reread some of my parents' books that dealt with that era? Did I like some of the other films he was getting a kick out of promoting, such as some of the great French and Italian classics including: *The Battle of Algiers, Touchez pas au Grisbi,* Fellini's *Nights of Cabiria* and Dassin's *Rififi.* He kept handing out DVDs for Lisette and I to watch and articles to read.

Bruce created such a buzz around *The Fallen Idol* that soon there were articles and pictures of me in *The New York Times* and *The Boston Globe.* Even the local press in my not-so-little town of Greenwich got excited. A reporter came to the hospital. I answered the usual questions: how did you get picked for the film, why did you act in just one and, by the way, what does a chaplain do?

Then *The Guardian* in London did a sympathetic and scholarly piece that, at least in my eyes, more than made up for the harshness of their 2001 article and enabled me to start thinking intelligently about how Graham Greene and Carol Reed had come together to develop the script. I do not know to what extent it was just a matter of chance but the BFI again got into the act and featured a picture of me on the cover of the hand-out for their 2006 summer festival, describing *The Fallen Idol* as 'possibly Carol Reed's greatest achievement'. I am in my pyjamas looking over the bannisters at the adults shoving and pushing each other, wrestling their way through their chaotic lives. It is the Graham Greene thing of looking at this confusing human mess and indulging in all kinds of thoughts including, or so I would like to think, whether there is a god and, if yes, then how exactly does he fit into all of this. For the first time I experienced real pleasure at the idea that all this grown-up wondering was being done through the eyes of a child.

Although I had been aware of the existence of *A Film Star in Belgrave Square,* the book my parents had worked on during the filming of *The Fallen Idol,* I had never read it. The title to this day makes me squirm and I had no desire whatever to be further drawn into anything to do with the film. It was only when I was well on my way to writing this book that I realised that I would have to face up to reading it – yet another piece of unfinished business – an elephant in the room, as it were.

I searched carefully through my father's books that are still in the room that was his study in his beloved Normandy farmhouse but found no trace of it: he must have purged it from his collection. By sheer luck, a couple my wife Lisette and I have known since our Oxford days had a copy in their possession. Both are doctors and Tom Arie, a distinguished psychiatrist and clinically obsessive frequenter of second hand bookstores, had picked it up in an East Anglian charity shop. Knowing I had embarked on a cathartic re-visitation of my prior life, he graciously gave it to me.

I read it not once, but over and over. I had already written the earlier chapters of this book based on my own, unprompted, memories of the making of *The Fallen Idol*. Rather than go back and add to what I had previously written I decided to treat this as a second look – a *The Fallen Idol* revisited. It was the oddest of feelings because it brought back incidents that I had either passed over as insignificant, or simply forgotten. Childhood memories are highly selective.

The book was published under my father's name and is written in the third person. There was, to me at least, something decidedly awkward about that since it is my mother's voice that comes through most of the narrative. In it, my mother is Madeleine (her real name) and my father is Philip, not Robert. Why the pseudonym? Why the need to distance himself from the whole experience? Does that not mirror the feelings I myself experienced as I grew up and found myself coping with what I can only describe as the real world? Towards the end of the book my mother recounts that Carol Reed asked her whether she wanted Bobby to be known by his own name or by a quite different one, to which she replies that he might as well keep his own. Why such a casual response, I ask myself today, to what surely was an important question? Might I not have also been in need of the same kind of distancing my father contrived to suit his own emotional needs?

The book was published in a hurry in early 1948 before the film's release later that year. It even refers to the film as *The Lost Illusion* rather than *The Fallen Idol*: a reminder of a last minute change that proved to be a good one. My parents had no way of knowing just how successful the film would turn out to be. On the first page they do in fact talk over the pros and cons of allowing their son to act in a film. Philip (my pseudonym-protected father) is reported as saying to Madeleine (my mother) that 'her dreams would be fulfilled in him (the child). His name instead of hers would burn across the city.' I am not entirely sure what to make of this startling statement heavy with psychological innuendos. I do, nonetheless, remember both my parents as very much taken up with the idea that fame is the ultimate prize held out to those who pursue literary endeavours – a promise of survival, albeit shadowy, beyond the grave. All very human, I suppose and I would never claim to be wholly exempt of such feelings.

The book deals with the question of money. A subject, as I have already observed, of inexhaustible interest to all of us. I know that. I am, after all, an accountant by profession. The contract stated I would be immediately entitled to £1,000 free of income tax. The free-of-income-tax stipulation was a big deal in 1947 given the extravagant rates of surtax imposed by the then Labour government. An extra £100 a week would be forthcoming if the shooting of the film continued beyond a certain number of weeks and, given Carol Reed's propensity for perfectionism, that would turn out to be a sure thing. No royalties, though, and that disappoints people who see reruns of the film on late night TV and feel I should be entitled to something. The book states somewhat quixotically that this bonanza would be placed in trust for the *child*. It was not! For the good reason that my parents needed the cash and that even in 1948 this was hardly a fortune. My father did feel a twinge of guilt because when he later inherited a bit of money at his mother's death he did set some of it aside for me. No hard feelings, but the subject did come up in my teenage years and gave rise to a few of those harsh parent-child exchanges that typify that ungracious phase of pre-adult life.

As a film star I was entitled to a stand-in. That sounds rather glamorous. Eric, my stand-in, was 15-years-old – almost twice my age – and was otherwise employed as a messenger by a sound recording studio. What a stand-in does mostly is act out the star's role during the hours it takes to set up the lighting and plan the camera's movements. This is tedious work that would unnecessarily wear down the star and increase the risk of cranky outbursts. Eric was apparently required to lean back on a shooting stick so he could come down to my height. He also had to put up with the indignity of having his hair dyed peroxide blond. He did play the on-location night time scenes where the child rushes down the Belgrave Square embassy's outdoor fire escape and then – terrified by witnessing what he takes to be the murder of the butler's wife – runs through the rainy darkened streets before being picked up by a policeman. Even though these scenes occur much later in the story, they were filmed right at the beginning. For good reason since the two studio sets – the basement room and the hall with the sweeping marble staircase where most of the film's action occurs – were still being built. I was slightly miffed – even back then – that I was not deemed tough enough to play those action scenes. Eric was paid 'two quid' a day, a quote from the book, for this work – a whole lot more, apparently, than what he earned as a messenger. The book does not say whether the daily £2 was a tax-free wage, but the realist that I have become knows perfectly well that there is no fairness in this world and that perks are only given to those who are already privileged and need them least. Do I remember Eric? The honest and somewhat embarrassing answer is hardly.

As a school age film star I was also entitled to a governess. That sounds decidedly less glamorous but my parents were pleased enough since it served to deflect criticism that they were botching their only child's education by not sending him to school like everyone else. My governess was of an indeterminate age, is pictured in the book in a dignified grey tailored jacket and skirt and went by the name of Mrs Cleverly. It would not have occurred to me back then that there was irony in a governess having the word 'clever' as part of her name. It turned out that she knew a lot more about the film business than teaching. When not holding herself out as a governess she made a living as a walk-on actress - an extra. My impression is that my mother regarded her as a useful source for the studio-related trivia that made its way into the book. She made me practise my lines and there was, undoubtedly, schoolwork involved but I don't think that made much of impression on me.

My mother appears in the film - for less than a minute. It is a long shot at the very end. The drama has at long last played itself out. It was, after all, an accident - ugly, admittedly, but not murder. The detectives have gone away. The idol that was once the butler is no more. Graham Greene has reduced him to a mere mortal, fallen - McGregor the snake has done his work - and booted out of Eden like the rest of us. As for the child, all that is left for him to do is to turn his back on the messiness and equivocation the grown-ups have brought on themselves, go back up the great marble staircase, away from the basement and from there to the nursery which is where he really belongs. Had his ambassador-parents not abandoned him over the weekend none of this chaos would have come about. Suddenly he hears a familiar voice calling out from the front door. He turns around - it is none other than his mother, the ambassador's wife. "*Viens, viens, mon chéri,*" she cries out in French. That's it - story over! One of the things I like about old films is the final title: THE END

My mother loved it. She was thrilled to have appeared in a real film. It was more than a walk-on part. She actually has a line and they didn't dub it. She experienced stage fright - the real thing - and even though I was off camera while she was being filmed they made me run up the stairs so she would feel less inhibited calling out at me. They had to do the scene again so there I am running up and down the faux marble studio staircase several times so she can get her one line right. It really is her voice. She made a big deal of it in the book. Carol Reed had the prop people rent a real mink coat for her - at a cost of £72, no less - and they brought it to the studio in a chauffeured car. This is the stuff of real filmmaking. In the 1950s and 1960s mink coats and diamonds were the heady symbols of fame and opulence. They also paid her £6 – maybe not a fortune but my mother loved the feel of crispy notes, and in 1948 an envelope containing six £1 notes was nothing to sneeze at. I, the jaded little devil I had become, was quite unimpressed by the insignificance of my mother's part and would have easily forgotten the whole affair. But no: the same people who ask me whether McGregor the snake was real and whether handling the creature put the fear of God into me also want to know whether the lady who appears in the last scene and claims to be my mother really is my mother. We love make-believe but the real thing also thrills us.

Then there is the haircut story. It is the kind of anecdote film buffs warm to. I suspect that savvy PR people spread around such stories to introduce a so-called human-interest element into the otherwise quite humdrum business of filmmaking. It was my mother's fault because she unthinkingly cut my hair at home over a weekend. That week a lot of time had been spent shooting an involved scene during the course of which I walk up the faux marble staircase. The shooting was to continue the following Monday and I hadn't finished going up the staircase. It came to be known as 'the world's most expensive haircut'. Do I detect a touch of bombast? Certainly, but it really was a major continuity mishap. There is a saying, so I read in my parents' book, 'that the camera sees everything'; that it can't be fooled. Nor would it have been possible, someone is reported to have said in jest, to introduce into the screenplay a haircutting session half way up the staircase. Paying a large studio staff to wait around while my hair grew back would certainly have been an expensive proposition. The story goes that the make-up crew had a go at gluing artificial locks onto my trimmed curls but that, frustrated beyond belief, I broke down in tears. Do you remember any of this, I'm asked? I don't, but that is hardly the point. It's a good yarn and it gave my parents a few extra pages for their book – something writers are always grateful for.

When I am asked what I remember most about the actual filmmaking, I invariably give as an answer that it was my fascination with its physical aspects: the set, the studio – all the things that contributed to the make-believe. My parents' narrative reminded me, however, that there was something else about the making of films that was totally new to me and almost as compelling. It was that the outcome of all this activity was the production of yards and yards of 35-millimeter celluloid film consisting of near identical images hemmed in on either side by endless edgings of precisely cut out little square holes. This was something refreshingly beyond the ordinariness of everyday life. The images themselves were sharp and bright and the thought that they could be blown up to cover a huge screen and be watched by a large crowd of people was awe-inspiring. It was thanks to this celluloid magic that moving pictures, or movies, are called films: that much I could grasp. The fascination began when I was first shown a 35-millimeter image of myself and invited to view it through a magnifying glass. I don't think it was just narcissism – although the fascination of self-contemplation manifests itself in humans from a very early age – but rather this thing of being invited to peer at reality through a strip of celluloid. At the age of eight I already had a keen sense that reality is something that can be made even more real by observing it through a looking glass. This went well beyond the magic lanterns of old because this succession of diminutive images could actually recreate movement. Maybe I already had a premonition that this was a way of perpetuating a moment that would otherwise have been forever lost; a stab at immortality – a magic lantern par excellence.

It *is* true because here I am in my 70s able to actually see people who are long dead move around and talk; or see and hear the child I once was and will never be again. I know that in the age of YouTube and digital imaging all that has become commonplace but back then there was something extraordinarily special about watching a rendering on celluloid of something that had taken place the day before.

My parents' book makes much of the fact that I was very taken with watching rushes, individual sequences of film projected in a small theatre-like room fitted out to meet the director's needs. This is where the director assesses each of the takes shot the previous day – developed and processed overnight by a specialised lab capable of producing positive images from the negative originals. Inside that little projection room the director is fully in charge. He is the true captain of the ship: the one who decides which of those sequences will make it to posterity and just how they will be cut and edited. He sits at a desk with a shaded light shining on his note pad, flanked by his assistants, his cameramen and his technicians. A director watching rushes has the heavy responsibility of deciding which scenes will have to be re-shot: a heavy responsibility because of the expense involved. Directors do not typically want to risk having opinionated self-conscious actors meddle with a process that is theirs by divine right. Actors are generally not welcome in this Holy of Holies.

There was therefore something special about being invited by Carol Reed to sit in the little theatre while the rushes were being projected. Why invite me? I think he had sensed just how curious I was. I am passionate about watching things from the outside: that is why I love travelling, watching a play, even dare I say so, watching a good film. More importantly, he probably reasoned that involving me in the process of filmmaking would make me more responsive to the task at hand – not consciously so, perhaps, but intuitively: that I would have a better sense of why he was asking me to do certain things in a particular way. Good psychology! To this day I am generally open to going along with what needs to be done but there is a strong independent streak in me that demands to know why. I can be difficult: polite, eager to please, but also mettlesome and easily bored by minutiae. I have every reason to believe that those character traits were a challenge to Carol Reed.

It had also slipped my mind that, stimulated by the practical side of film-making, I began to create my own films. These 'films' consisted of rudimentary sequences of parallel frames featuring stick figures drawn on glued-together narrow gauge strips of paper. As in the silent films, the actors spoke to each with the help of written frames – used sparingly and in my case most often grossly misspelt. I have the impression that Carol Reed encouraged this tinkering and that he shrewdly reckoned that anything that drew me into the mysteries of filmmaking suited his higher purpose. The plots in my rudimentary creations had nothing remotely to do with *The Fallen Idol*: I was no Graham Greene! What appealed to me were the battle scenes and the sword fights I had witnessed during the making of *Bonnie Prince Charlie*. My imagination ran to knights in armour jousting within sight of crenellated castle walls. I must have had something of a 'castle and moat' complex because the studio carpenters even built one for me. Those were the stories that in my view were really worth immortalising.

Then there was the model theatre I was given for the Christmas of 1947 and a reminder that it was by now obvious that the making of the film would extend well beyond the three months originally contemplated. This was an honest-to-goodness model theatre equipped with proper red velvet curtains, battery-powered dimmable stage lights and scaffolding from which to hang scenery, backdrops, wings and all manner of props. I was delighted: this was a copy in miniature of a real thing that was itself a make-believe world peopled by actors that, the moment they climbed onto a stage became, magically, people other than whom they really were. I was so taken by the magic that, years later, I made an eerily similar one for my own children. I had completely forgotten, though, that it was a gift to me from Sir Ralph Richardson – that greatest of Shakespearean actors who, with Gielgud and Olivier, had rejuvenated the Old Vic. That was the part, though, that really interested my parents and caused them to mention it in their book.

The book prompted my remembrance of the camera – my camera. There was nothing fancy about it. It had a lens with a couple of stops and a fixed-speed shutter, but I liked the feel of it. It was small, had sleek, pleated, retractable bellows, and even smelt good. It took film tightly wound on a spool, and the number printed on the film's paper backing was legible through a small red round disc at the back. That was the only way of telling how many exposures were left. That was the way cameras worked. It was mine to play with and I knew it hadn't come from my parents because they had absolutely no interest in gadgets. I don't remember either of them ever taking a picture... not ever. We really were a strange family. It wasn't until I read their book that I became aware of how it had come my way.

There is a huge difference between the person who produces a film and the one who directs it. Carol Reed was on the set every single day directing what everyone did down to the smallest gesture. Sir Alexander Korda was 54 at the time and had done his fair share of directing – numerous films both in Europe and in Hollywood: some inspired and brilliant but many others abject box office failures. He was, though, an entrepreneur by temperament and his days as a director were over. Now he was the producer, but not just any old producer. He was the undisputed 'big boss', the owner of London Films – remember Big Ben, booming, triumphant and steadfast, introducing each of his films – and when it came to money and choosing the best people money could buy it was Korda who called the shots, every single one of them. I can't say that as a child I was aware of much of this but, yes, I did sense that he was the 'big boss' behind the scenes. He would appear from time to time – *deus ex machina*, to use an apt theatrical term – bearing gifts such as oranges for the worker bees toiling on the set. It felt, and indeed was, highly paternalistic. My parents' book does a fine job evoking that feeling. I also sense that a gentle, condescending pat on the upcoming child star's fair head and the proffering of a few honeyed words of encouragement – Korda had a reputation for being a charmer and not just with the ladies but with anyone from whom he was determined to wheedle a favour – were part of the act. So, according to my parents' book – my sole source for such high-class trivia – that December, Korda invited me, in my parents' company of course, to what they referred to as a 'Christmas tea'. It was a private tea, no less, since we were the only guests. The tea was held in Korda's suite at Claridges located on the top floor of the fabled hotel. It was the great mogul's inner sanctum. Over apparently scrumptious tea-cakes, Korda spoke of his childhood: of his father, in particular, who had managed a vast wheat-growing estate in the fertile central plain of what is now Hungary but was then very much part of the Hapsburg Empire. My parents delighted in every minute of it and couldn't help noticing a Monet – two young women reclining on a punt – and in the hallway studies of dancers by Degas. It was at the conclusion of this tea that Korda presented me with a gift-wrapped box containing the little camera. I remember nothing of the tea and had also forgotten who had given me the camera. I am humbled by the selectivity of my childhood memories.

Today, looking back at those distant events through the lens of my parents' book feels understandably strange. I was playing the kind of games eight-year-old children undoubtedly play but doing so within an exclusively adult world. Eric, my 15-year-old stand-in was a companion of sorts but certainly not a playmate. It is fair to say that the only child that I was had no contact with anyone remotely my age. The people who watched my 'films' and my 'plays' were adults. They were my critics and inclined, out of self-interest and politeness, to indulgence and easy praise. I sense that to my parents there was something intensely pleasing and flattering about such a state of affairs. They were like gardeners taking pride in growing a lush, precocious plant in a heated winter garden. 'In spite of it all he's growing up quite normal,' they would say reassuringly to themselves, 'neither spoilt nor demanding'. Those are the sentiments I see reflected in the back-and-forth between Madeleine and Philip as they dialogue in *A Film Star in Belgrave Square*. I have no desire to blame my parents for any of this and I do, in a certain way, feel lucky to have had such an unusual experience, and yet! I think the 'yet' has to do with the fact that when eventually I was confronted with reality – the devastatingly unvarnished mockery that so characterises the manner in which the young vie with each other – I was alone and totally unprepared. It was as sudden as it was harsh. It was then that I unceremoniously cast off what felt like embarrassingly conspicuous and unwanted baggage. In time I recovered a lot of what had been ditched in such a hurry – the good parts hopefully – but the recovery itself took place over many years and brought about its own form of pain. It was as if my awareness of the past had been numbed by a far too long-lasting anaesthetic.

the fallen idol

advertising...
publicity...
exploitation

Epilogue

Even now it is not quite over. I have friends who have an uncanny flair for ferreting articles that pop up quite unexpectedly one side or another of the Atlantic.

Mark Romanek, the producer of *Never Let Me Go*, wrote in the summer of 2011 in the *Daily Telegraph* something that was so shocking to me that it almost sent me back to my previous state of yearning for anonymity: '*I was immediately hooked by Bobby Henrey's performance of the boy Philippe – even to this day its naturalism is unparalleled. I think it's the greatest unpolished child performance of all time.*'

There was more. The 2012 New Year edition of *Newsweek* has Meryl Streep on its cover in her rendering of Maggie Thatcher. Inside Martin Scorsese, glowing from his success in producing *Hugo* – a film I greatly enjoyed – gives his take on the ten best films ever featuring children. Surprise... surprise *The Fallen Idol* is among them. Here's what Scorsese has to say: '*A uniquely frank picture about a boy negotiating his way through the adult universe, from Carol Reed (who worked so well with children) and Graham Greene, with great performances from Ralph Richardson and Bobby Henrey as the boy.*' I liked that. The business about negotiating my way through the adult universe is right on – I am still at it!

The old idea that this whole thing would in time just fade away had obviously not worked. My wife had been right in saying to me all along that I might as well just enjoy it. It was high time I begin looking at it all through grown-up eyes.

Postscript

Where Are The Snows Of Yesteryear?

Are we not all naturally curious to know what has happened to people we have known in the distant past but have lost sight of? We are especially interested in finding out about children for they do indeed have a way of growing up and vanishing. That is probably why people like peppering me with questions about *The Fallen Idol*. Now, however, it was my turn to want to find out about everyone else involved in the making of the film.

Thanks to the 2001 encounter at the BFI, I had actually met two of the survivors. The remaining known survivor – the fourth, oldest, and most probably best known – is, of course, Michèle Morgan. She had not accepted the BFI's invitation to come to London. There was really nothing surprising about that. I like to think of her as the *grande dame* of French cinema and so I doubt she gives much thought at this late stage of her life to her erstwhile association with this quintessentially British period piece – surely slightly quirky when seen through French eyes. Besides, I do remember her as ever so slightly distant. Anyway, London can be quite dreary in late November.

That said, the remarkable thing about Michèle Morgan is that at the time of the making of *The Fallen Idol* she was only 28 and yet had already acted in the two films for which she will always be best known – the first being *Quai des Brumes*, director Marcel Carné's 1938 masterpiece. She plays tough guy Jean Gabin's passionate yet perplexing lover. Her other claim to enduring fame was playing the part of the blind girl in the 1946 film version of André Gide's *La Symphonie Pastorale* who, having recovered her sight, is confronted with wrenching and irreconcilable emotional conflicts. It is not that she gave up acting at an early age. Far from it! It is just that none of her numerous subsequent films – mostly French – ever really matched her earlier successes; at least not internationally. In 1950, she married

Henri Vidal, who was reputed to be the most handsome French actor of his time but, beset by depression, died of an overdose at 40. Widowed, she went on acting, successfully took up painting, and in the 1970s published a thoughtful autobiography. She was recently photographed celebrating her 90th birthday. In the picture she is blonde, radiant, dignified, ramrod straight, and is cutting her cake surrounded by admiring grandchildren. It is an image fully consistent with the memory as an eight-year old child I have of her well on my way to sensing the magic and mystery conjured up by the presence of a beautiful, even if somewhat distant, woman.

What of the others? We, the very few survivors, are moving up that escalator from which we also will soon be required to step off – gently, we hope. All the others, so far as I can tell, have one way or other already been nudged off. The only way I could satisfy my belated and newly aroused curiosity was to turn to my computer. I am no professional historian and am grateful to the likes of Wikipedia for offering such a wealth of information to the merely inquisitive. I did my searching this last August in what I have referred to as the ancient farmhouse of my birth. I feel lucky that it is still around for me and for my family and that this remarkable phenomenon we call the Internet is capable of passing through its much-weathered walls.

Ralph Richardson died in 1983 of a stroke at 81. In many ways he, Carol Reed and Graham Greene formed the trio that was really responsible for the making of *The Fallen Idol*. He was the oldest of the three but not by much: Graham Greene was born a mere two years after him, and Carol Reed was only four years his junior. Carol Reed was actually the first to die – of a heart attack in London in 1976 at the relatively young age of 69 – and Graham Greene turned out to be the longest lived of the three.

Ralph Richardson earned his place in history as one of the all-time giants of the London theatre scene: he was up there with Laurence Olivier and John Gielgud. He also played leading parts in a staggeringly large number of films: more than 80 from 1933 to 1983, the year of his death. He was, of course, already famous, when he was chosen for the lead role in *The Fallen Idol*: he was already Sir Ralph, having been knighted that very year. He was indefatigable, and cinema buffs might remember him in some of his later success, *The Heiress* (1949), *Our Man in Havana* (1959), *Doctor Zhivago* (1965), and even *Greystoke: The Legend of Tarzan, Lord of the Apes* (1984). I did not warm to the Tarzan story but recognised him in the others as the patient and consummate professional who had graciously put up with me as a fidgety eight-year old.

Richardson briefly considered joining the Jesuits: ever so briefly because he is said to have absconded from the seminary in the dead of night. He was once quoted in a newspaper article as saying that thanks to his Catholic upbringing "... I think I must be influenced by ritual, because I believe there's a kind of religious sense in what I do. I think actors, rather like priests, have a sense of what can be done by ritual." It goes without saying that this is the kind of thought I warm to.

Richardson was, apparently, fond of animals and as I wandered around the Internet in search of anecdotes came across this one: He was found by the police one night walking very slowly along the gutter of an Oxford street: he explained he was taking his pet mouse for a stroll. There are also reports of Sir Ralph indulging his inner fantasies by riding on a motorbike with a parrot on his shoulder. It does me good to get to know these people even if more than 60 years have elapsed since I first met them.

A year after *The Fallen Idol,* Carol Reed went on to produce *The Third Man.* It was clever, elegant, and haunting in its evocation of the dark, chastened mood of post war Europe. Its crisp black and white images and soulful zither music contributed to creating a mood that made it into the all-time cult film for lovers of the refined film noir genre. It also made Reed into one of the most acclaimed producers of his generation and established Graham Greene's narrative style as one that was pre-eminently suited to filmmaking. Once more, Reed was able to have his pick from among some of the best known actors of the day, namely Joseph Cotton and Orson Welles. It was the very same Welles who had masterminded *Citizen Kane* in the early 1940s, considered by many to be the greatest film ever made. So overwhelming was Welles' reputation that Reed never fully shook free of the probably unjustified rumour that Welles was the true genius directing *The Third Man* from the side lines.

The Fallen Idol had been voted Best British Film of the Year, and Reed had received the New York Film Critics Award for directing it, but this was as nothing compared to the acclaim surrounding *The Third Man.* It received awards such as the Grand Prix de Cannes and, much later in 1999, was declared by the British Film Institute to be the best British Film of the 20th Century. Reed was knighted in 1953.

Ten years later, Reed and Graham Greene came together once more to make *Our Man in Havana* (1959), a tongue-in-cheek film in the noir tradition that delights as it sets out to debunk the idiosyncrasies of the British Secret Service. Reed continued to make films and some, such as

Outcast of the Islands (1951), The Agony and the Ecstasy (1965), and *Oliver* (1968) achieved distinction. It is, however, the three films he made in quick succession in the post war years that are generally viewed as most representative of his remarkable talent: *Odd Man Out, The Fallen Idol,* and of course, *The Third Man.*

At the time *The Fallen Idol* was filmed, Graham Greene was only 43: his career as a novelist and as a writer with a particular affinity for filmmaking continued up to his death in Switzerland in 1991. He was well into his 80s reconciled, some say, with the Church with which he had been at odds for most of his life. He was a highly prolific and often controversial novelist whose stories reflected his own struggles with the presence of evil and the role of grace within the human condition. He also wrestled with the politics of the cold war and of imperialism: in particular with the corrosive effect of colonisation on countries such as Mexico, Cuba, Haiti, Liberia and Vietnam. He experienced bouts of acute depression. Complex, brilliant, delighting in paradox, tainted I am told by an anti-Semitic streak, and utterly driven by the urge to express his ideas through the characters he created for his countless novels, he formed relationships with artists and writers among whom were Charlie Chaplin, François Truffaut, and Evelyn Waugh.

Beyond this brilliant trio there were others associated with *The Fallen Idol* who met with subsequent success: Jack Hawkins, in particular, who had played the relatively minor part of one of the detectives investigating the death of the butler's wife. It was his success as the lead in *The Cruel Sea* (1952) – a film based on Nicholas Monsarrat's thoughtful novel on the futility of war – that made him one of the outstanding British film actors of the 1950s and 1960s. He acted with Alec Guinness in *The Bridge over the River Kwai,* and was given the role of General Allenby in *Lawrence of Arabia.* He was a heavy smoker and died at 63, probably of throat cancer.

There was also Sonia Dresdel who played the part of both villain and victim – the Queen of the Night, as it were, of *The Fallen Idol.* It is of her that I have the fondest memories. She was unfailingly kind and seemed to take genuine interest in me as a person. A sympathetic critic said of her that notwithstanding her terrific personality she was, during the latter part of her career 'terribly underused and misused'. She earned a living out of numerous minor parts in TV productions and died in 1976 aged 66. That is as much as I could find out about her. What sadness! I would have wished her a lot more success and a long happy life.

Finally I remember Denis O'Dea, the senior police inspector who plays a key role in the film's closing scenes. There was something calming and comforting about his presence on the set that probably had much to do with the reassuring softness of his Irish lilt. He had met his wife Siobhán McKenna at the Abbey Theatre in Dublin. He died in 1978 aged 73: that's how old I am as I write these lines. So much for the moving escalator!

Acknowledgements

I would not have undertaken this revisitation of my past without the encouragement of wise and supportive friends. Joe Mehan was the first to suggest it - kindly but firmly. I'm thankful to the others who also contributed to overcoming my reticence - among them Nico del Castillo, Tom Arie, Sean O'Connor, David and Susan Rounds and Bill and Jeannemarie Baker. Thank you also to Foster Hirsch, Kevin Brownlow, and Robert Moss for agreeing to read the manuscript and generously sharing their in-depth knowledge of the film business and sound critical judgement. I'm especially grateful to Jerry Johns without whose editorial guidance, tenacity, and good sense the endeavour would have foundered. He was fortunate in engaging the services of Fiona Thompson whose painstaking editing of the final text has enhanced it; and in obtaining permission from David Rayner to use photographs from his collection of *The Fallen Idol*. Then there was Bill Schneider who insisted I persevere. reminding me that there is nothing easy about the business of writing. The last acknowledgement concerns my long suffering wife Lisette who also read early versions and made a lot of helpful suggestions and whose repeated advice to me that I just get over this Fallen Idol thing I finally heeded.

[*All photographs and images are from the author's private collection unless otherwise stated.*]

Index